Praise for *Unleashing Excellence*

"In the restaurant business, achieving and maintaining excellent customer service is of paramount importance. *Unleashing Excellence* is a must read that would benefit any industry. It gives step by step guidelines that can be implemented with ease and invaluable insights that will help encourage your customers to keep coming back for more instead of leaving before the first bite."

—Fred DeLuca
President and Co-Founder Subway Restaurants

"If your organization is not fully committed to service excellence, don't read this book. If you are fully committed, then you MUST read this book. It provides all the nuts and bolts of how to create and sustain a service culture."

—Pamela Paulk
Vice President, Human Resources Johns Hopkins Health System

"Business in the early twenty-first century has turned into a survival game—those who figure out how to keep their customers survive. If you need a customer service improvement plan and don't know where to start, START HERE! Teri Yanovitch and Dennis Snow have put together a thorough guide for building a successful customer focus strategy in an organization of any size. In a plan of only 9 steps, *Unleashing Excellence* shows step-by-step how to build the business case for customer focus and service improvement, supported by successful business examples, guidelines and worksheets, and accountability strategies and measurement plans. The plan is logical, the book is easy to read and non-technical—highly recommended."

—Tom Willett
Director, Management Development Programs
Cornell University, ILR School

"There is no shortage of books extolling the importance of excellent customer service. What distinguishes *Unleashing Excellence* from the others is its focus on how to do it. If you are convinced of the value of service excellence and want to know how to provide it, this book is for you."

—Allan R. Nagle
Former President, Tupperware Worldwide
Former Interim Dean, Crummer School of Business, Rollins College

"Customer service is key to the success of any company. I recommend *Unleashing Excellence* to any company needing a 'how to' and 'can do' manual to implement service excellence in their organization."

—Richard A. Nunis
Retired Chairman, Walt Disney Parks & Resorts

"Dennis Snow and Teri Yanovitch have once again authored an easy-to-read guide, rich with real-life examples of companies striving to achieve customer service excellence. We started following the simple 'how to' steps described in *Unleashing Excellence* (first edition) in June of 2004. 'Everything speaks' and 'through the lens of the customer' has changed our approach to providing great customer service. The second edition is a must read as it expands the concepts and steps necessary to take an organization to new customer service heights. In this incredibly competitive world, following these concepts will improve your business and your personal life!''

—Gary Webb
Executive Vice President—Operations
First Financial Bankshares, Inc.

''Once again, the authors have pinpointed the dynamics of the changing nature of delivering customer value through a focus on excellence. Wise words for any organization to heed.''

—Dr. Robert K. Prescott, SPHR
Graduate Faculty of Management Rollins College
Crummer Graduate School of Business

''Few books written on the topic come close to the kind of thoughtful examination of the customer psyche that I've read here. Dennis and Teri seamlessly marry the intangible tenets of customer service philosophy with practical, easy-to-consume strategies that can help any organization transcend 'business as usual.' The authors illustrate their recommendations of 'what to do' with stories that make it easy to understand. And, *Unleashing Excellence* does not just tell us *what*, it shows us *how*.''

—Chuck Kegler
Director, Kegler, Brown, Hill & Ritter

''If your organization wants to make customer service a part of your culture, *Unleashing Excellence* is a powerful tool. The authors, with their keen understanding of what it takes to accomplish this in any business, walk you through understanding the process and the commitment that it takes to be successful. It is truly a step by step 'how to' guide. If this model can help a government agency reach a 93% overall customer satisfaction rating, it can help any organization. The book also helps anyone who reads it understand that excellent customer service isn't a 'program' but a 'process' that never ends.''

—Kimberlee Poulton
Director of Communications and Marketing
Florida's Turnpike Enterprise

UNLEASHING EXCELLENCE

The Complete Guide to Ultimate Customer Service

Second Edition, Updated and Expanded

Dennis Snow
Teri Yanovitch

To Jennifer & Charlie
With my best wishes!
Teri Yanovitch

WILEY

John Wiley & Sons, Inc.

Published by John Wiley & Sons, Inc., Hoboken, New Jersey.
Published simultaneously in Canada.

For general information on our other products and services or for technical support, please contact our Customer Care Department within the United States at (800) 762-2974, outside the United States at (317) 572-3993 or fax (317) 572-4002.

Wiley also publishes its books in a variety of electronic formats. Some content that appears in print may not be available in electronic books. For more information about Wiley products, visit our web site at www.wiley.com.

ISBN: 978-0470-50380-5

Printed in the United States of America

10 9 8

Contents

Preface to the Second Edition

Since the release of *Unleashing Excellence* in 2003, the world of business has gone through some dramatic changes. The global economy suffered an unprecedented blow, forcing governments, businesses, and consumers to re-evaluate priorities and scramble for ways to solve the situation and ensure it doesn't happen again. The quality and ethics of leadership have been universally questioned, and many once high-flying companies collapsed under the weight of corporate greed, faulty business models, and misplaced priorities. The total disregard for customers by a handful of unethical companies destroyed the financial lives of countless people.

We wrote *Unleashing Excellence*, however, for those organizations that *do* care about their customers and want to create an environment that demonstrates that care. This book is written for those organizations and those leaders who want to make a positive difference in the lives of their customers and their employees—and reap the financial benefits of doing so.

It comes as no surprise that the business landscape has become even more challenging since *Unleashing Excellence* was originally released. In addition to those issues already addressed, some of the most dramatic changes are the result of:

- The increased commoditization of most products and services. For nearly every dollar they spend, consumers have more choices than ever.
- The accelerated growth of the Internet. Already a strong presence in 2003 when this book was first released, online businesses have become a dominant player in many industries. Whereas the mom and pop specialty retailer in Burlington, Vermont, used to compete with the competitor across town, now it's competing with the competitor in Bangalore, India. Or with the eBay entrepreneur operating out of the basement in her house.
- The almost total access consumers have to information. A prospective customer, client, patient, resident, or passenger can learn all they want to know about your organization and your products and services from the comfort of their own homes. The oft-cited statistic that a dissatisfied customer will tell nine other people about their negative experience is grossly out of date. Through blogs and consumer advocate web sites, unhappy customers can *instantly* reach an audience of millions and share the details of their frustration.

These, as well as other changes, have made a comprehensive, strategic focus on creating a culture of service excellence more important than ever. The value of earning customer loyalty through a carefully orchestrated service experience is only going to increase in the future.

Positive feedback from readers of *Unleashing Excellence*, as well as from our consulting clients, has validated that the process outlined in this book works. Increased customer satisfaction, increased employee satisfaction, and improved business results have been reported to us. Readers have shared specific customer "wow" stories that were inspired through the disciplined application of the principles discussed in the book. The most common comment we receive from readers is that *Unleashing Excellence* is the only resource they've found that lays out a service

improvement process in a step-by-step approach, making implementation simple (but not easy!).

Not all of our clients and readers, of course, have achieved the
dramatic results they had hoped for. While disappointing, there is
something to be learned from the unsuccessful attempts at
applying the book's principles. Comparing the successful appli-
cations of the *Unleashing Excellence* process with the unsuccessful
ones yields four critical factors that are at the heart of those
improvement efforts that did achieve their objectives.

1. The successful initiatives had unwavering commitment
   from the senior executive team—the CEO in particular.
   The senior executives were intimately involved in the planning and execution of the initiative and were relentless in
   their pursuit of service improvement. Their "failure is not
   an option" approach to the initiative virtually guaranteed
   its success.
2. The successful initiatives were launched with an understanding that significant change doesn't happen overnight.
   The leaders understood that each step in the book is
   important and that this is a process, not a quick-fix program. We've seen impatience doom many service improvement initiatives. A long-term commitment is needed in
   order to achieve the benefits of the process outlined in
   the book.
3. The successful initiatives did not focus on "fixing our
   frontline employees." The leaders recognized that it
   must be an all-encompassing approach that not only
   focuses on employee behaviors, but also on processes,
   structure, internal relationships, and ultimately on leadership performance. Creating a culture of service excellence
   is the responsibility of management. The current level of
   customer care in an organization is a direct reflection of
   management priorities.
4. The successful initiatives built accountability into the
   process, and no one and no entity was exempt from

participating. Service excellence ultimately became *non-negotiable* at every level of the organization. Tools for timely corrective action were implemented so that poor customer service, internal or external, was not tolerated.

In addition to the success factors just described, we've learned other things since the first release of *Unleashing Excellence,* and we've included those lessons in this new edition. We've provided some updated tools as well as some new ones. We've shared best practices from clients and readers who've taken the principles and adapted them to their particular situations, along with their suggestions for successful implementation. And we've included our own observations of what works and what doesn't from our consulting engagements. Customizable copies of the forms and tools presented throughout *Unleashing Excellence* can be downloaded from www.UnleashingExcellence.com.

Although the second edition of *Unleashing Excellence* contains plenty of new or updated information, the purpose of the book remains the same as when it was first published. Our purpose is to provide you with a step-by-step manual for raising the bar of service in your own organization. We're confident that, if you follow the process described here, you'll create customer experiences that separate your organization from the rest of the pack and will lead to intense, "walk-through-fire" customer loyalty.

Acknowledgments

Writing and publishing a book is a challenging endeavor; one that requires the combined efforts of many other people besides the authors. Without the contributions of those listed here (and many more, we're sure), this edition of *Unleashing Excellence* wouldn't have seen the light of day.

First, we'd like to sincerely thank those clients and individuals who provided the case studies and examples used to bring the *Unleashing Excellence* principles to life. Thanks to the teams at Machias Savings Bank; Cummins (and their many entities); Cool Cuts 4 Kids; First Financial Bankshares; LYNX; Florida's Turnpike Enterprise; Naugatuck Savings Bank; Georgia Southern University; The Bartlett Group; Texas Bank and Trust; Walt Disney World; Community Blood Center of the Ozarks; First Citizens Bank; Westgate Resorts; Seminole Community College; and Springfield Clinic.

We are deeply indebted to our editor, Lauren Lynch, and the rest of the team at John Wiley & Sons, Inc. It has been an honor and a pleasure to work with such a prestigious publisher, and we appreciate the care and attention you've shown.

To name all of the friends and colleagues who have supported us over the years would be a dangerous task since we would undoubtedly leave someone out who should be recognized. But, please know that we cherish your friendship and your contributions to whatever success we've enjoyed. We feel truly fortunate.

And most importantly, we thank our families—you have had the greatest impact of all on our work and on our lives. To George, Melissa, Michael, Debbie, Danny, and David; we thank you for your love, patience, and support. You make everything worthwhile.

Introduction

I just wanted a quick bite to eat, so I stopped at a fast-food restaurant. Thought I'd go inside rather than do the drive-through. None of the people working the customer counter looked happy, but hey, I'd be in and out. When it was finally my turn to order, a truly bored employee gestured for me to speak.

"I'll have a cheeseburger and a medium drink, please."

"Mmph plfs wpl chlef?" She mumbled, never making eye contact with me.

"I'm sorry, what was that?"

"Mmph plfs wpl chlef?" she mumbled again, a little louder this time, still no eye contact.

I was getting embarrassed. "I'm sorry, I'm not understanding you."

"Do—you—want—fries—with—that?" this time with eye contact that clearly communicated that she thought I was a moron.

"Uh, no thanks." I quietly answered, trying not to make her mad.

She put my burger and drink on a tray, pushed it toward me with no comment, and went on to the next customer. As I walked away I heard her ask the next customer, "Mmph plfs wpl chlef?"

Scenarios like this one are all too common. The service provided by most companies is mediocre at best, atrocious at worst. How many times have you quietly (or not so quietly) fumed over slow, rude, inefficient, indifferent, or inept service? Chances are strong that you've suffered poor service many times—*this week*. But those few organizations that *consistently* provide excellent service, demonstrating that they truly care about their customers, are our heroes. They provide a safe haven from the usual storm of service aggravation. And they are very rare. The big question is—why are excellent service providers so rare?

Excellent service is rare because it takes real *commitment* to make excellence "business as usual." The service concepts themselves are not complicated or difficult. The level of commitment required is the hard part. A service improvement initiative is similar to an exercise program. The beginning is exciting. You buy exercise equipment or join a health club, buy workout clothes, and read about exercise routines and healthy living. The first few workouts are invigorating and you feel good. Then, other things begin to take priority. You skip going to the gym or taking your run. Each time you skip a workout it becomes easier to skip the next one. Soon your running shoes are gathering dust in the closet or your gym membership lapses. Most people repeat this cycle over and over. Only those individuals who are *truly* committed to sustaining a healthy lifestyle are willing to put in the work of running when it's raining, working out when they are tired, or eating a healthy meal when a Big Mac is a 5-minute drive away. The same is true with creating a culture of service excellence. Many organizations begin a service initiative with banners, speeches, and rallies, only to allow the initiative to die a quick death when the real work begins. Most organizations don't truly commit to building a lasting service culture.

Our purpose in writing this book is to provide a *step-by-step guide* for planning, implementing, and perpetuating a service culture in your organization. Many of the customer service books out there spend much of the book explaining *why* customer service is important. Our assumption in writing this book is that you are already convinced about the whys. What is needed are the *hows*. This book is a how-to manual for creating service excellence. The order of the chapters is important. Each element of the process described is important. The chapters will guide you through the process of gaining involvement and "buy-in" throughout the organization and will detail the systems that need to be put in place. Creating a service culture involves all functions and all levels of the organization.

One thing is certain: Creating a culture of service excellence is certainly *not* a matter of telling employees to "be nice to customers and smile." Some employees (like the one in the opening story) just don't care. These employees have no business being in the service industry. In many cases, however, employees are doing the best they can with the tools available to them. When company policies get in the way of service, customers and employees are often the victims of a "non-service" culture. The airline gate agent who can't give you a straight answer regarding a delayed flight doesn't have the *mechanisms* she needs in order to provide you with the information. Surely, most gate agents would *love* to be able to make you happy. Their jobs would be much more pleasant that way. Without the proper mechanisms, however, there is nothing the gate agent can do. Over time, she puts up an emotional barrier in order to protect her dignity. To the customer the gate agent appears indifferent. Nobody wins in such cases—not the customer, not the gate agent, and not the organization. World-class service providers, on the other hand, see excellent service as the responsibility of the entire organization, and they build a culture to ensure that world-class service is delivered.

Some businesspeople still think of customer service as fluff. For these managers, service is too soft to pay serious attention to. To them, customer service is simply smiling and making eye contact. Conversely, stellar service performers see focusing on the customer experience as a vital component of their success formula and incorporate it into everything they do. From the way employees interact with customers, to the user-friendliness of their processes, to the design of their facilities, these organizations make customer service excellence a priority. And they reap the benefits of doing so. Consider the following statistics:

- A study conducted by BIGResearch for the National Retail Federation and American Express found that 85 percent of consumers shop more often and spend more at retailers that offer higher levels of customer service. Eighty-two percent said they are likely to recommend retailers with superior customer service to friends and family.
- Eighty-seven percent of banking customers who experienced positive "moment of truth" experiences increased the value of products purchased or purchased new products altogether (McKinsey Quarterly, 2006 Number 1).
- In research conducted by the Journal of Marketing, an investment in a stock portfolio based on high scores as reported by the American Customer Satisfaction Index (ACSI) between 1997 and 2003, a volatile time in the market, the high customer satisfaction portfolio outperformed the Dow by 93 percent, the S&P 500 by 201 percent, and the NASDAQ by 335 percent.

This book is for those companies that want to be known for service excellence. It provides principles and techniques that will endure in the long run. Excellent service is not an add-on; it is imbedded in the way exceptional organizations deliver products and services—every time, with every customer. It is not a program that has a lot of hype in the beginning and then fades away. This is a process; it does have a beginning, but not an end.

A large multinational corporation, or a small, locally based organization can implement the approach presented in this book. The principles are the same; it's just the scope that changes. If you run or are a part of a small company, the Service Improvement Team and subteams discussed in Chapter 3 may not be appropriate. The functions and activities discussed in the chapter, however, are appropriate. Focus on the principles and tools;

adapt the execution to your world. We have seen these concepts succeed in a small, 24-bed hospital as well as in corporations with thousands of employees.

When leaders of excellent companies are asked for the secret of success, one word shines through: commitment. Over and over in our consulting work, we've found that service improvement initiatives led by senior leaders who are relentless in their commitment to the initiative's success far outperform those led by senior leaders who pay lip service to the effort but aren't engaged in the actual work. The engaged senior leaders recognize the need for long-term commitment and know that, if their own commitment falters, the rest of the organization will follow suit.

Creating a culture of service excellence takes time. We live in a society, however, that wants change to happen immediately. We want results now! Lasting change doesn't work that way. As described previously, anyone who has successfully sustained an exercise program knows that you work, work, and work without seeing the physical benefits for quite a while. Then you notice that you're beginning to tone up and are getting stronger with more endurance. Later, other people start noticing your progress and ask how you did it so quickly. Right. If they only knew. With a service improvement effort, you need to do the upfront work before you see the results. You'll see some progress along the way, but the big results manifest themselves down the road. This delay is why most organizations begin and abandon one improvement program after another, similar to the reason why most people abandon one exercise program after another. Both are hard and take time. Those organizations that stick with it are the ones who become world-class.

Since this book is a how-to manual, read through it with a highlighter and pen available and mark those areas where you know your organization is struggling. We have tried to supply many tools to help you with the process, so you are not starting from scratch. As ideas that are applicable to your organization come to you, jot them down in the page borders. If you own or lead a small business or organization, we again caution you to not disregard certain concepts because they appear suited for only large companies. The ideas in this book apply to *any* organization—you may simply need to adapt the execution of the idea. Customizable copies of the forms and tools presented throughout *Unleashing Excellence* can be downloaded from www.Unleashing Excellence.com.

Pay attention to what other companies are doing to deliver excellent service. No matter the company or the industry, you can always learn from excellent performers. Pull together an influential team of people from your organization and discuss the strategies and tactics discussed in the book. Start to look at ways you can implement these ideas so that customer service becomes a key component of what your organization is known for.

Remember, though, that unless you are starting a new business, changing a culture takes 3 to 5 years. Don't be impatient; it will happen if you stick with it. Changing behaviors and current ways of doing things is rarely easy. And, while it takes time to form new habits, once these habits are in place, it becomes hard to remember how "we used to do it." Aristotle once said, "we are what we do repeatedly, therefore, excellence is not an act, but a habit." This book will help you to make excellent service a habit.

Chapter One

THE DNA OF SERVICE EXCELLENCE

"I hate furniture shopping, almost as much as I hate car shopping. But my husband and I decided that we needed new furniture for the living room, so we dragged ourselves to a local store. I went in with my fists up, ready to fight off all the pushy salespeople. I'd dealt with pushy salespeople before. Walking around the store, however, I felt different there. The salesperson was helpful but didn't hover. When we had a question, he magically appeared. Everything about the store felt good. I still can't put my finger on it. We bought our furniture there without looking anywhere else."

It's a challenge to define excellent service because it's a feeling that you get. You know it when you get it, and you know it when you don't. This chapter, however, will provide a framework for defining excellent service for your organization. We're going to look into the "DNA of service excellence." The concepts, language, and examples in this chapter will provide the groundwork for everything to come later in the book.

"Inculturating" Service Excellence

You won't find the word "inculturate" in any dictionary, but it accurately describes the whole purpose of this book. The idea is for excellent service to ultimately become part of your company's culture. You want employees to perform in an excellent manner because such performance is part of the organizational DNA.

Let's imagine, for example, you're in a restaurant and you observe an employee interacting with a customer. The employee is providing outstanding service and going to great lengths to ensure that the customer is satisfied. Imagine approaching this employee with: "I'm impressed with the way you served that customer. What gets you to give great service like that?" The best answer the employee could give is, "I'm not sure what you mean. That's just the way we do things here." A response like that means that the behavior is simply the normal course of business. Contrast that response with one such as, "Well, management has video cameras monitoring us, and if we don't act happy we get in trouble." This type of answer indicates an initiative based on coercion, not organizational DNA.

The Framework

Many (if not most) organizations overcomplicate any initiative they try to take on, including service improvement initiatives. These organizations analyze everything to death and end up paralyzed—too overwhelmed to do anything. The approach recommended in this book is designed to be simple and straight-forward. It takes commitment, but it's not complicated.

"Simplicity is the ultimate sophistication."
—Leonardo da Vinci

Figure 1.1 gives you a snapshot of the framework for service excellence. It is based on our observations of outstanding, service-

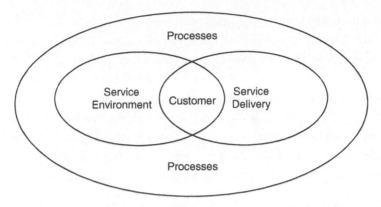

Figure 1.1   Customer Service Model

driven organizations and our analyses of the activities that make these organizations great. We've also studied the not so great to analyze what's missing. Four components make up the framework: the Customer, the Service Environment (physical setting), the Service Delivery (employees), and the Processes.

You'll notice that the customer is in the center of the framework shown in Figure 1.1—the customer experience being the driver of the service strategy. The service environment and service delivery components overlap the customer component since they are designed from the customer's perspective. Finally, the processes component surrounds everything. Effective processes ensure that each element of the model is executed in an excellent and sustainable manner. Let's take a closer look at each element.

The Customer

Most organizations say they put the customer at the center of everything they do. Experiencing the service they provide, however, quickly blows that theory. Their processes and policies demonstrate that the focus is on *their* convenience, not the customer's. We've all been frustrated, for example, by phone trees that say; "For sales, press 1; for reservations, press 2; for customer service, press 3." For real customer service we shouldn't have to press anything; we should get to talk with someone right away! They've made things more efficient for themselves, but they're irritating customers in the process. The situation has gotten so bad that several consumer web sites now offer secrets for bypassing phone trees. GetHuman.com, for example, provides specific codes callers can enter in order to get to a live person at hundreds of organizations. GetHuman.com has to update the site regularly because companies keep changing the codes in order to keep customers from getting through. It's a sad situation.

The Lens of the Customer

A truly customer-focused organization sees things through the "lens of the customer." This approach asks, "How does the *customer* see us?" Looking at the operation from the customer's perspective is one of the performance elements that separates outstanding organizations from ordinary ones. Customers appreciate the difference.

If you've ever tried to navigate the corridors of most hospitals, you know that the signage doesn't usually offer much help. It doesn't help because staff members who already know their way around the hospital designed the signs. Arrows pointing in 40 different directions make sense to people working in the hospital every day. Those of us who only visit the hospital in stressful times find that these directional signs only add to the stress. The designers weren't looking through the customer's lens.

Common employee statements that indicate a lack of looking through the customer's lens include:

- "The computer won't let me do that."
- "First, I need you to fill out this paperwork."
- "I'm not sure if we carry that item. If we do, it's on aisle 5."
- "My department doesn't handle that. You'll need to call xyz department."
- "Have a seat; someone will be with you."
- "I'm closing this restroom for cleaning. There's another one on the next floor."

These statements aren't blatantly rude; they simply indicate a company focus, not a customer focus. Even a seemingly innocent statement such as, "I'll have someone call you right back," indicates a lack of seeing through the customer's lens. What constitutes "right back" for one person is probably different for another person. Is it 5 minutes, 15 minutes, or an hour? Nit picking? Not to a customer waiting by the phone for you to call "right back." What about the furniture store that tells you that the delivery truck will be at your house between noon and 5 PM? Whose convenience are they concerned with? Whose lens are they looking through?

Understanding the Customer's Lens

A very simple method exists for discovering the lens of the customer. Once you discover this lens, you're able to perform accordingly. You may be tempted to disregard the method because it's deceptively simple. Don't disregard it. It works. The method is this: *If you understand the customer's **emotions**, you will understand the customer's **needs**.* Customer emotions are the key to personalized service. The following two possible statements by a visitor to a hospital provide clues to the customer's emotions:

- Statement 1: "I'm here to see my daughter. She just had a baby. Can you tell me what room Sally Jones is in?"
- Statement 2: "I'm here to see my daughter. She was just in a car accident. Can you tell me where I can find Sally Jones?"

These two statements reflect completely different situations and, therefore, completely different emotions. Unfortunately, both customers will probably be treated in exactly the same clinical manner. While this example may seem extreme, similar situations happen regularly. Is the situation of the young couple taking out their first mortgage the same as that of the person who buys and sells real estate regularly? A completely different emotional dynamic exists. The young couple is nervous, overwhelmed, and excited. They need understanding, clear information, and a banker who is visibly happy for them for taking the big step of buying a house. The experienced real estate buyer has very different emotions and, therefore, very different needs. Yet many lenders will treat these situations the same way.

Computer help-lines are notorious for not understanding the emotions customers are dealing with. When you have a computer problem you're frustrated and anxious. You have work to do! Computer help-line phone trees are long and complicated, and most customers don't understand the nuances of the different options anyway. When you finally do talk with a technician, they use "computer speak." You become more confused and frustrated as the process goes along. Those rare times when you get a technician who speaks in normal, everyday language, you feel comfortable and appreciative. It's just a change in approach—the excellent companies understand the emotions and needs of their customers.

As you implement the customer service tools and techniques recommended in this book, it's important to constantly remind employees to see things through the customer's lens. Using this lens as the decision-making compass dramatically increases the likelihood that your improvement efforts will succeed. Focus the lens on customer emotions and needs. You might hear the argument, "What if we're wrong about the customers' emotions? We can't read their minds!" Yes you can. By shifting the mindset to the lens of the customer, employees will read the situation correctly most of the time. What about those times they're wrong? When an employee is truly trying to understand the customer's situation and respond to his or her needs, the employee is likely providing great service even though he or she may have read the customer's emotion incorrectly.

A bank client shared the story of a teller at the bank's drive-through window who noticed the customer she was serving was in tears as she pulled up to the window and placed her deposit slip in the container. It was clear that the customer was fighting back sobs as she waited for the teller to complete the transaction. As she placed the customer's receipt into the container, the teller also included a short handwritten note expressing her hope that whatever was wrong would turn out okay. The customer gave a grateful smile as she drove away. Did the teller overstep her bounds? We don't think so. Our position is that it's better to provide an outstanding, caring experience and perhaps periodically misread the situation than to make the decision to be mediocre for everyone in order to avoid any missteps.

In Chapter 4, you'll be introduced to Service Mapping—a tool used to ensure that each step of the customer experience is designed with the customer's lens in mind.

The Service Environment

Imagine yourself in a restaurant. As you sit down, you notice the table is a little dirty. There's something crusty on your fork. How comfortable would you be? Wouldn't you start worrying about what else might be wrong?

Everything Speaks

Every detail of an organization's physical environment is saying something about their brand. Everything the customer sees, hears, touches, smells, and tastes creates an impression—"everything speaks." Customers may not consciously pick up on every detail, but, make no mistake about it, an impression is made. Overflowing trashcans, empty display shelves, peeling paint, and burned-out lights all speak to the quality of the overall business. A bank ATM, for example, is an expensive piece of technology. How many times have you walked up to an ATM only to see a crudely handwritten out-of-order sign taped to this expensive piece of equipment? If everything speaks, what does this sign really say? Go away! Certainly that's not the message that was intended, but it is the message received. Everything speaks.

Making sure that the setting is right is a sign of respect for the customer. The everything speaks philosophy also has a subtler meaning. If a company can't handle the small details, why should the customer believe that the company is capable of handling the big, important details? A customer's experience renting a car illustrates the point:

"I needed to rent a car for a fairly lengthy stay in Chicago, so I reserved a car through one of the bigger name rental companies. When I walked into the office, the first thing I noticed was a roll of toilet paper sitting on the customer counter (this should have been the first indicator of how I was going to be treated). I just couldn't take my eyes off that roll of toilet paper as I tried to figure out why it was there. The service rep finished his conversation with a fellow worker before finally making eye contact with me. As he apathetically went about the necessary details, I looked around the office at the various stacks of paper, used coffee cups, and dirty office fixtures. I felt more and more like this was a fly-by-night operation, yet it was a name we all know. The rep finally directed me to my car. After loading my bags in the trunk and adjusting my driving directions, I turned the key and . . . nothing. Realizing that I had probably turned the key incorrectly, I turned it again . . . nothing. I proceeded to unload my bags and trudge back to the office only to be treated (by the same representative) like I hadn't been there four minutes earlier: 'How can I help you?' I explained that the car wouldn't start and he looked me dead in the eye and asked, 'So, you don't want the car?'"

That roll of toilet paper on the car rental counter was an indicator of bigger problems. Again, if a company can't handle the little details, what makes us think it can handle the important details (like cars that start)?

Getting your employees in the everything speaks mindset is a critical component of the service improvement effort. Every employee needs to take personal ownership. Everyone, beginning with the boss, must enter the business as a customer and be alert to *any* negative messages delivered by the appearance of the organization's environment.

Raise the level of awareness by noticing and talking about elements of the physical environment that detract from the company's image. What do these negative elements say to the customer? What does a dead plant in a doctor's waiting room communicate to the customer? What does a dirty glass in a restaurant communicate? What does a messy desk in a banker's office communicate? Make no mistake, something is communicated—everything speaks. Just raising the level of awareness helps to focus attention on the details.

One leader we know used a creative technique to focus his team on the quality of the physical environment. Tired of constantly seeing trash scattered around the facility, he implored his employees to pay more attention and to make an effort at keeping the place clean; but nothing seemed to work. In a team meeting he asked the employees why they didn't pick up the litter. "Because we're so busy, we don't even see it," was the response. So, before the next team meeting, he scattered a few crumpled dollar bills throughout the facility and watched with quiet amusement as his employees picked up every single bill. In the next team meeting, he explained what he had done and what he had observed. The issue wasn't one of being too busy to see the trash; the issue was one of being motivated to pick it up. They got the message.

Leadership, of course, must set the tone by walking the everything speaks talk. Leaders can't just tell employees to pay attention to the details while ignoring the same details themselves. Employees quickly see through such hypocrisy. When employees see a member of management walk by a piece of trash, not picking it up, a clear message is sent. A very different message is sent when employees see the boss take the time to pick up that piece of trash. Some of the best training comes from leaders modeling the values of the organization. Employees are watching to see what's important to the boss.

Bob Gillikin, former president of Cummins Southern Plains, placed a heavy focus on the everything speaks philosophy in his diesel sales and service operation. He knew he had to set the right tone for his team. Bob actively participated in keeping the facilities looking great by picking up litter and helping to eliminate clutter. And he was also willing to invest money where needed, whether in painting facilities, re-striping the parking lot, or purchasing new displays for the distributorship. His investment of time and money clearly communicated that it was everyone's responsibility to ensure the environment conveyed a positive message.

Observing employees who have developed the everything speaks mindset is gratifying. Any time one of these employees sees something out of place they handle it automatically. It becomes part of who they are. That type of behavior is indicative of an organization that has inculturated service excellence.

One of the tools described in Chapter 4 is the Everything Speaks Checklist. This tool helps to ensure that the physical environment positively reflects the organization's brand.

The Service Delivery

No matter what business you're in, customer service success ultimately comes down to your people. Even if your business is the epitome of automation, it still takes people to design and maintain that automation and to formulate your business strategy. Service delivery encompasses the people element of your organization. Successful service delivery is driven by employees performing in such a way that your customers not only want to come back, but they *automatically* come back. You don't want your customers to even consider doing business with the competition, do you? You want your service to be so good that customers enthusiastically recommend your company to others. Customer referrals are as good as it gets. In his studies of customer satisfaction survey questions most closely correlated with referrals and repeat purchases, noted researcher and business author Fred Reichheld states in his book, *The Ultimate Question: Driving Good Profits and True Growth* (Harvard Business School Press, 2006,

p. 26), "It turned out that one question—the Ultimate Question—worked for *most* industries. And that question was, 'How likely is it that you would recommend Company X to a friend or colleague?'" So how do you achieve this level of service? Create "service wows."

Create Service Wows

Some of you may have rolled your eyes when you read the words, "Create service wows." You may have thought, "If one more book tells me I have to wow customers, I'm going to scream." The reason for this feeling is that the examples cited are always huge, grandiose gestures of service generosity. Examples:

- The employee who drives his personal car through blinding snow to deliver a pair of shoes to a customer so that the customer has just the right shoes for a holiday party.
- The employee who arranges first-class upgrades for every step of a newlywed couple's first trip (ever) out of their home state.
- The employee who cheerfully gives his own watch to a customer who has lost his watch.

These are all actual examples and represent wonderful service. But how many organizations can consistently do these things and stay in business? When we speak of creating service wows, we're talking about small things, consistently done, that please the customer. The bank teller that puts a dog biscuit in the drive-through container when she notices a dog in the car. The flight attendant who assists a passenger who's struggling to find over-head bin space. The theme park employee who approaches a visitor who clearly needs directions, rather than waiting for the guest to ask. Each of these examples represent small, seemingly insignificant behaviors. Imagine, however, a corporate culture in which *every* employee does these small things in the normal course of business. The impression that results is one of service excellence that makes customers say, "Wow." It also makes customers want to come back.

The two arguments we often hear about creating service wows are:

1. *"If we do these service wows consistently, won't they eventually become expectations?"* Yes. And that's a wonderful thing. If you routinely do things that your competitors don't, you become a beacon of light in an otherwise dark customer service world. Your consistency of excellence becomes the wow. Don't worry about it until your competitors start catching up. And, if you've built a culture of service excellence, your employees will always be looking for new ways to wow customers, so you'll stay ahead of the game anyway.

2. *"Customer expectations are too high as it is. It's too tough to please them."* Bull. Customer service is so bad that most of us have learned to expect nothing. Anything that a company does that is special, even if the employees just smile at us, is like a gift. A company that uses the "expectations are too high" argument is simply looking for an excuse to stay mediocre.

What can your organization do to create service wows? The best way to figure that out is to sit down with employees and talk about it. Most employees have done something that wowed a customer, and some have techniques they use regularly. Pulling together a group of employees to talk about service best practices starts to leverage these wow techniques. As employees listen to the stories of others they often will think, "I can do that." It simply takes an effort to weave certain behaviors into the everyday life of the organization.

One organization looked at the way they handle incoming phone calls that need to be transferred to another department. In the past, the customer would have to explain the problem again to the next employee in the chain. In order to provide a customer wow, even when a call had to be transferred, the team agreed to stay on the line with the customer to smooth the transfer. The original employee answering the call would introduce the customer and the situation to the employee who would handle the call. Customers now feel like they're dealing with one organization, not a group of disconnected individuals. And since they're not used to that kind of service, they're probably thinking, ''Wow.''

Chapter 4 will introduce the Service Philosophy and Service Standards, which help guide employees in wowing customers in ways that are consistent with the organization's brand and can be done at little or no cost.

Processes

The final component of the customer service model is the ''processes'' component. Again, note in Figure 1.1 that the processes element surrounds all of the other elements. Processes are the magic key for inculturating service excellence. Many service problems have nothing to do with employee attitudes—they have everything to do with broken processes.

''I had a customer who wanted to exchange a television set that he bought and decided he didn't like. Even though he had his receipt, our store policy is that the manager needs to approve all exchanges on merchandise over $400. I kept paging the manager but got no response. I tried to be friendly, but the customer kept getting madder as time dragged on. I really couldn't blame him. My manager finally showed up and took two seconds to approve the exchange. The customer got what he wanted, but he wasn't real happy about the experience.''

Service Heroes

Effective service processes *set employees up to be service heroes.* An example drives this point home. Walt Disney World cast members are expected to know the answers to all guest questions, right?

You logically know that this is impossible. There is no way for a Disney cast member to know everything. So a mechanism has been put in place to assist. This mechanism, called Information 4500, is a central phone number (4500) that any cast member can call with a guest question they can't answer. Information 4500 keeps a database of the questions and answers so that cast members can answer questions ranging from "What time does Epcot open tomorrow?" to "How many bricks are there in Cinderella's Castle?" (None—it's made of fiberglass.) Guests are impressed with the cast's ability to answer the questions, and cast members feel supported in being service heroes. Everyone wins.

It's one thing to tell employees, "go out and give great service." It's another to be committed enough to put the processes in place that allow for great service to be provided. This kind of commitment separates the world-class organizations from the "wannabes." Chapter 10, The Service Obstacle System, is an entire chapter dedicated to identifying process issues and developing customer-focused solutions.

Concluding Thoughts

In this chapter we've looked at the framework of a service-driven organization—the DNA of service excellence. Imagine if everyone in your organization consistently applied each element of the framework. Every employee would look at the operation through the lens of the customer. Customers would feel your employees understand them. You would see employees paying attention to the details of the work environment because they know everything speaks. Customers would know they're dealing with a quality organization. Employees would consistently do those little things that create service wows. Customers would feel special and cared for. Finally, you would see an organization that is constantly improving and looking for ways to create service heroes. What a dynamic work environment that would be!

We've already mentioned some of the tools you'll learn about in future chapters. In fact, the rest of the book is about creating an organizational culture that makes each of the principles described in this chapter, "business as usual." These principles are the foundation of a culture of service excellence:

- See everything through the *lens of the customer.*
- Pay attention to the physical environment because *everything speaks.*
- Provide service delivery that will *create service wows.*
- Develop processes that make employees *service heroes.*

Chapter Two

THE LEADERSHIP ACTIONS

"We went to a customer service seminar last year and brought along the entire management team from our division. The sessions were great. The concepts that the speakers discussed were right on target, and they gave us time to think about how to apply the concepts to our business. Networking with other companies and hearing how they handle some of the same challenges was helpful, too. I took lots of notes. But when we got back to work we got caught up in the day-to-day activity and never applied what we learned. We've done nothing different since attending the seminar. Nothing."

Most organizations have detailed plans that outline how they will increase revenue, profits, and market share. They spend weeks or months putting together precise operating budgets every year. Few organizations, however, put anywhere near the same amount of effort into planning how they will improve customer service and retain the precious customers they already have. Customer service improvement remains an afterthought or a "back burner" initiative for some future time.

It's no wonder that few organizations actually succeed in making *lasting* improvements to their approach to customer service.

Chapter 1 introduced the basic service concepts:

- See everything through the *lens of the customer.*
- Pay attention to the physical environment because *everything speaks.*
- Provide service delivery that will *create service wows.*
- Develop processes that make employees *service heroes.*

The purpose of this chapter is to help apply structure to your service improvement efforts. Many service initiatives stall because they rely upon good intentions, not a disciplined approach. This chapter introduces the process used to inculturate the service concepts examined in Chapter 1; the rest of the book expands on each component of the process. In the end, you'll have a complete roadmap for bringing your service initiative into existence or to a higher level.

Ensuring that service excellence becomes part of the culture takes effort. Some of the activities involved are high profile and energizing, while others are more difficult and perhaps even mind numbing. Most organizations are quite willing to do the splashy, energizing components of a service improvement initiative. Few companies, however, are willing to dig into the details of *all* organizational processes and make changes to the organizational DNA. Sustainability of a service improvement effort requires a well-thought-out, coordinated strategy that is supported with tremendous commitment in terms of time and attention. Without long-term commitment, it is likely that another "flavor-of-the-month" program will begin and eventually end. Flavor-of-the-month initiatives are demotivating to everyone. Chances are you can think of plenty of flavor-of-the-month programs your own organization has suffered through.

We're calling the elements of the improvement process "Leadership Actions." This phrase was carefully chosen because we recognize that most stalled initiatives are based on leadership *desires.* The anecdote at the beginning of this chapter is one example of leaders who desired change but didn't take action to implement change. Leadership Actions are exactly what the phrase implies—actions that need to take place to create change.

Each Leadership Action plays a vital role in the process. Leaving out any one of them will cause a gap in the improvement effort, resulting in reduced effectiveness. Some of the Leadership Actions may feel comfortable, while others may feel awkward at first. We once heard someone remark that following the Leadership Actions was similar to learning to drive a stick-shift car. At first, you probably had to think through each action. You were probably uncomfortable and likely stalled the car several times. You may have even considered giving up because you couldn't imagine ever becoming comfortable coordinating all of the actions. With time and practice, however, the awkwardness began to disappear and soon you didn't have to think about the individual actions—you were simply driving the car. It's the same with the Leadership Actions. You have to stick with each one to get through the awkward stage.

The Nine Leadership Actions

1. Create the Service Improvement Team (Chapter 3).
2. Develop the organization's service improvement core tools (Chapter 4).
3. Develop and execute an ongoing service communication and awareness plan (Chapter 5).
4. Create and execute a plan for ongoing service training and education (Chapter 6).
5. Adapt the interviewing and selection processes to include all elements of the service culture (Chapter 7).
6. Create and implement a service measurement process (Chapter 8).
7. Develop appropriate recognition/celebration processes that reinforce the service culture (Chapter 9).

8. Implement a service obstacle system for identifying and addressing barriers to service excellence (Chapter 10).
9. Build an accountability system that ensures commitment to ongoing service excellence (Chapter 11).

Rigorous application of and adherence to these actions will ensure that *your* service initiative isn't another flavor-of-the-month program. In this book, each of the nine Leadership Actions has a dedicated chapter in which we'll discuss the action in detail and provide recommendations for implementation. We'll provide examples from our own experiences along with lessons learned, stories shared, and tools discovered.

Concluding Thoughts

As you read the following chapters, keep in mind that the service principles presented in Chapter 1 are at the core of the entire approach. The Leadership Actions bring the principles to life. Working your way through each Leadership Action will help your organization define its own excellence and inculturate that excellence.

Small organizations may be tempted to skip one or more of the Leadership Actions. We ask that you carefully consider each action and adapt it to your company's size. It's similar to aircraft design: There is certainly a difference in the complexity of a jumbo jet versus a twin-engine propeller airplane, but the fundamentals of getting and keeping the plane in the air are the same. Each of the Leadership Actions in this book are fundamental to the success of any service-driven organization.

Chapter Three

THE SERVICE IMPROVEMENT TEAM

This chapter focuses on the first Leadership Action: creating the Service Improvement Team. It's a tough chapter because it describes setting up a committee, and most of us don't like committees. But the Service Improvement Team can be the catalyst that makes your service initiative have a *lasting* impact. Many service improvement initiatives begin with the best of intentions but fade away because no mechanism is put in place that ensures the activities needed to truly inculturate the service principles are in place. The Service Improvement Team is that mechanism and drives the entire process described in this book.

Watching a world-class sports team as they practice can be enlightening. They go through lots of drills as an entire team, but they also focus on their own specialties. The objective is to create a cohesive team while capitalizing on the strengths of the individual members. Not an easy task. You'll notice as you watch these teams practice that there are numerous coaches. The coaches each work with one or more of the athletes, trying to attain flawless execution of their specialty. But the coaches also work from a team playbook, ensuring that everything is linked and part of a cohesive strategy. The coaches get together often and talk through team strengths, weaknesses, and opportunities. When watching team sports on television, we mostly see the head coach; but they can't do the job all by themselves. All of the coaches are important to building a world-class team.

The function of the Service Improvement Team is similar to that of a group of coaches. The members of the Service Improvement Team take on different responsibilities of the service initiative, but they also make sure that all activities are part of a cohesive, well-planned strategy. This team gets the initiative going and ensures that it keeps going. The Service Improvement Team concept is flexible. In large organizations, the team concept is appropriate. In a very small organization, it's possible that one or two people can manage all of the functions described in this chapter.

Note that this group is *not* called the Service Improvement Police. They are also *not* called the Service Improvement Serfs. Their job is not to issue commands and demand compliance. Nor is it their job to do all of the work. Instead, like a group of coaches, they facilitate the service improvement effort. They work with the organization to capitalize on strengths, help develop service improvement strategies, and ensure that all of the activity is linked. Without such a core team the service improvement effort could go in a hundred misaligned directions, or it will more likely go nowhere at all because of a lack of attention. The members of the team change over time, but the team itself never goes away. It will always be there to ensure that customer service remains a priority.

Make-Up and Responsibilities of the Service Improvement Team

An organization's Service Improvement Team is usually comprised of 8 to 10 senior-level individuals representing a variety of organizational functions, along with an administrator (described later in the chapter). Senior-level authority allows members the ability to remove roadblocks to the process, which is especially important at the beginning of the initiative. Decisions must be made, approved, and executed efficiently, without a lot of bureaucratic red tape and approvals. Input and involvement will come from *all* levels of the organization, so don't worry that service decisions will come down from the "ivory tower." As time goes along, it is appropriate to involve others on the team, but the first Service Improvement Team needs to have the authority to get things done.

Your actual number of team members will depend on the size and complexity of your organization. For example, a credit union we worked with consisted of 40 employees covering three branches. Their Service Improvement Team consisted of the general manager, the marketing manager, and the three branch managers—just five members. Similarly, a grocery store's team might consist of the store manager, assistant manager, and department managers. Keep in mind that a team of more than 8 to 10 members can be unwieldy. One organization we heard of created a committee of 40 members. Imagine the difficulty of scheduling meetings, hearing all ideas, reaching consensus, and making decisions. It's likely that nothing got done. Later in this chapter we'll discuss some special situations that might require a creative structure for the Service Improvement Team, but our experience has shown that a team too large is much worse than a team too small.

The Service Improvement Team is a part-time job for most of the members; they fulfill their Service Improvement Team responsibilities in addition to their regular duties. However, for large organizations, the administrator position may turn into a full-time job. Typically, the members of the first Service Improvement Team are in place for 12 to 18 months. Thereafter, half the team changes over to new members each year.

Each Service Improvement Team member champions one or more of the Leadership Actions. For example, the champion of the Training and Education Leadership Action makes sure that appropriate service training is developed for all employees, new hire orientation is revised to include key elements of the service culture, and ongoing training is planned and executed. This champion makes sure that the training is linked to the overall service improvement effort. He or she is accountable to the Service Improvement Team for the planning, implementation, and communication of the training. This is a big job! Consequently, most champions create subteams that concentrate on the appropriate Leadership Action. The subteam is typically made up of content experts (including frontline employees) who understand what it takes to actually implement the Leadership Action. Continuing with the Training and Education example, the subteam may be made up of members of the Training Department and trainers from all over the organization. The champion ensures that the work of the subteam fits into the overall strategy. We'll describe the subteams later in the chapter.

While the nine Leadership Actions don't roll out in a strictly linear timeframe, certain activities do take place early in the process while others occur later. Communication about the initiative, for example, naturally begins before significant work on the Service Obstacle System or Accountability Leadership Actions take place. Don't allow the Service Improvement Team to operate in silos, with some champions sitting back waiting for earlier work to be done. Yes, each Leadership Action has a champion, but it's one team in which members involved with later activities assist with those immersed in earlier activities—and vice versa. We want to emphasize the importance of treating the work as a team effort! Make sure this is understood from the very beginning.

Here's how to set up your Service Improvement Team. Keep in mind that this structure is provided as a template; you'll likely need to make adjustments to fit your organization. The main thing is to make sure that things get done in an effective and cohesive manner. Figure 3.1 provides an organizational chart of a typical Service Improvement Team.

Chairperson

The Service Improvement Team chairperson is the champion for Leadership Action 1, meaning that this individual is responsible

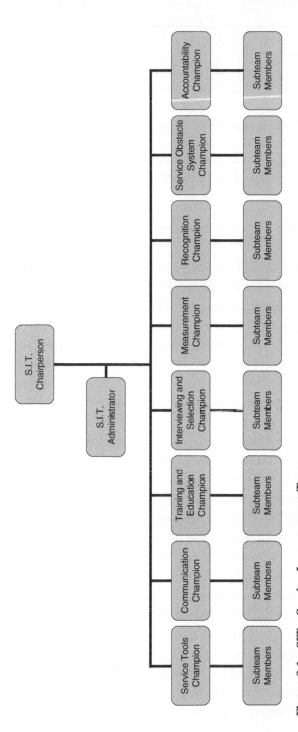

Figure 3.1 SIT—Service Improvement Team

Note: This organizational chart depicts one Leadership Action per member. In actual practice, a member may champion more than one Leadership Action, thereby reducing the size of the Service Improvement Team.

- Develop Service Improvement Team meeting agendas with the help of the Administrator.
- Run the Service Improvement Team meetings.
- Report progress to the Board and other company executives.
- Ensure communication is flowing to the entire organization.
- Keep the Service Improvement Team focused and accountable.
- Remove roadblocks to the process.

Figure 3.2   Responsibilities of a Chairperson

for leading the team. Figure 3.2 outlines the responsibilities of the chairperson.

The chairperson should be the most senior member of the Service Improvement Team, especially in the first year. For some of our client engagements, the president or CEO stepped into the chairperson role. Whatever you decide, a top executive Service Improvement Team chairperson sends a strong message regarding the importance of the service initiative and dramatically increases the likelihood of its success. It also raises the level of accountability regarding the team members' commitments. As Bob Gillikin, former president (and Service Improvement Team Chairperson) of Cummins Southern Plains, told us, "The leader can't just see this as a front-loaded process where he just says 'do it' and then steps away. The leader has to be personally committed and personally involved throughout the entire process. I was accountable, the Service Improvement Team members were accountable, and the entire Cummins Southern Plains organization was accountable for the success of this effort. The consistency of our combined efforts made it work."

The success of the Cummins Southern Plains service initiative was (and continues to be) stunning. Their success has been due to having the right people on the Service Improvement Team with a "failure is not an option" mindset. Whoever your chairperson is, he or she must be supremely committed to the improvement process, be a risk taker, and, most important of all, *possess the ability and authority to get things done.*

Administrator

Think of someone in your organization who seems to have a special ability to coordinate and stay on top of a variety of cross functional activities and details—someone who's able to somehow keep everyone informed of what's going on and understands how to get around the bureaucracy in order to get answers and take action; someone who, for some reason, really enjoys doing all of the above. That person would be the ideal Service Improvement Team administrator. In a large or complex organization, the administrator *may* be the one person assigned full time to the Service Improvement Team. This individual has a lot to do to make sure everything is coordinated. Figure 3.3 outlines the responsibilities of the administrator.

The administrator can best be described as a project manager and shouldn't have responsibility for any specific Leadership Action. Just staying on top of all of the activity and keeping communication flowing will be a big job. This person must be detail oriented and able to handle a lot of information. It's a critical position, so look for someone who loves this type of work.

Keeping track of deadlines and commitments is a significant part of the administrator's job, and Figure 3.4 provides an example of a tracking sheet (abbreviated) that the administrator can use to track all of the activities. It's a living document, with

---

- Work with the Chairperson in developing Service Improvement Team agendas.
- Handle the logistical details of all Service Improvement Team meetings.
- Record all discussions and decisions from the Service Improvement Team.
- Follow up on all team member assignments to track progress and ensure completion.
- Develop and administer a master document that tracks all aspects of the service improvement process.

Figure 3.3   Responsibilities of an Administrator

June Report — 7/24 Conference Call

Action Items	Progress Report	Due Date	Comments/Challenges
Communication – John Smith			
1 Newsletter article written by CEO introducing the service initiative.	Article will be ready for September newsletter.	July 31	On track.
2 Posters with logo, Service Philosophy/Standards communication kit sent to all branches and departments.	Kit components complete. Will send out when dept. heads are updated on their responsibilities.	July 31	New date for distribution is August 15th, following the department head meeting.
Training and Education – Jane Johnson			
1 Put together training subcommittee.	Getting input from SIT members. Two recruits at this point.	June 19	Suggestions for members needed by end of week.
2 Schedule employee workshops and communicate schedule to the field.	Schedule complete. Will be distributed following initial company-wide communications.	June 22	On track.

Figure 3.4 Service Improvement Team Tracking Sheet (Go to www.UnleashingExcellence.com to download a customizable copy of this form.)

Measurement – Bill Watson			
1	Review current service quality measurements.	Meetings with departments to identify current customer service measurements.	July 1	List of all current service quality measurements.
2	Develop branded measurement charts to distribute to field.	Meeting with vendor to produce the charts. Have sent logo.	July 15	On track.
3	Develop baseline measurements that will track overall impact.	Meeting with executive team to discuss key measures.	July 10	Determine 3-4 overall organizational baseline measurements.

Figure 3.4 (*Continued*)

completed activities dropping off of the tracking sheet over time and new commitments being added. Using a tracking sheet such as the one shown will make the administrator's role much easier than simply trying to keep track of commitments based solely on meeting minutes. While Service Improvement Team meeting minutes should also be kept, the tracking sheet will be the primary mechanism for ensuring that team members follow through on their commitments.

A word of warning regarding the role of the administrator: We often see the administrator role abused by other members of the team. Because the administrator regularly touches all of the Leadership Actions and tracks what's being done, it's easy for this person to get sucked into the minutia of scheduling training programs, distributing measurement charts, tracking recognition programs, and potentially hundreds of other activities. It's not that the administrator can't assist with some of these responsibilities; the problem arises when the administrator role becomes a dumping ground for activities other members of the team should be doing. The chairperson should be watching for any signs of administrator overload. One client's administrator quickly became a one-person Service Improvement Team—and just as quickly became overwhelmed as members abdicated their work to her. We reminded the chairperson that he needed to step in and stop the inappropriate "delegating."

Service Improvement Team Members

If the chairperson is the head coach and the administrator is the team manager, the Service Improvement Team members are similar to assistant coaches. They're involved in the overall strategy development and will champion one or more of the Leadership Actions. Members typically select a Leadership Action that aligns with their individual area of responsibility or expertise. In some cases, a member takes on a Leadership Action because of a passion for the subject, such as employee recognition. Figure 3.5 outlines the responsibilities of Service Improvement Team members.

- Attend all Service Improvement Team meetings.
- Participate in Service Improvement Team decision-making.
- Champion one of the Leadership Actions.
- Create a subteam to develop and implement action plans for the appropriate Leadership Action.
- Maintain ongoing communication with the Service Improvement Team regarding plans, progress, and challenges.
- Represent his or her job function in the Service Improvement Team decision-making process.

Figure 3.5   Responsibilities of Members

Clearly, all Service Improvement Team members must have a passion for service excellence and demonstrate long-term commitment to the process. Each member must be counted on to follow through on assignments and responsibilities.

Creating a Team Charter

A team charter provides the Service Improvement Team with a clear sense of mission and a set of operating guidelines. Figure 3.6 provides a template that should help you get started developing your own charter. Some organizations have viewed creating a charter as unnecessary and then later regretted not taking the step to create one. You may think that everyone is clear on the direction of the group but later find out there are misunderstandings regarding commitments and responsibilities. Creating a charter at the beginning eliminates a lot of headaches later on. Signing the charter signifies that each member understands what the Service Improvement Team is all about and what's expected of the membership.

Service Improvement Team Meetings

You probably feel that you already have too many meetings to attend, and you probably do. The following note was anonymously sent around one organization:

PURPOSE:
To design the plan, provide training, and implement the Service Improvement Process at [company name].

MEMBERSHIP:
The first Service Improvement Team will be comprised of the highest level of authority in each of the major areas of operation in the organization; in addition, an administrator will also serve on the team. The members of subsequent Service Improvement Teams are nominated by the current Service Improvement Team and approved by the senior executives. The chairperson of subsequent Service Improvement Teams will be selected by the CEO and also appoint an administrator. Members are expected to serve for a minimum of one year.

TEAM RESPONSIBILITIES:

1. Set the direction for the service improvement initiative.
2. Document the role and responsibilities of the members, chairperson, and administrator.
3. Assign a Leadership Action to each Service Improvement Team member.
4. Determine time schedules and goals for each Leadership Action.
5. Ensure consistency of all Service Improvement Team plans with the business objectives of the organization.
6. Review and approve plans developed by all Service Improvement Team subteams.
7. Coordinate Service Improvement Process plans and assist areas with implementation.
8. Observe the progress, successes, and challenges resulting from implementation, and make adjustments as needed.
9. Designate a succession plan for turning over the Service Improvement Team into the next service improvement cycle.

INDIVIDUAL RESPONSIBILITIES:

1. Attend all Service Improvement Team meetings or provide a representative. Be prepared for all meetings.

Figure 3.6 Sample Service Improvement Team Charter (Go to www. UnleashingExcellence.com to download a customizable copy of this form.)

2. Follow through on all commitments made as champion of one of the Leadership Actions.

3. Create and lead a subteam for the purpose of developing and implementing the strategy of the assigned Leadership Action.

4. Assist other team members as needed.

5. Be an ambassador of the service improvement initiative.

MEETINGS:

- Meetings will be held biweekly initially, then monthly.
- Meetings may be held via teleconference if needed.
- Meetings will be conducted following an agenda published by the administrator in advance of the meeting.
- The administrator will record all decisions and actions on a tracking sheet. Meeting minutes will also be kept as a record of discussions that take place. The tracking sheet and meeting minutes will be updated and distributed to all members of the Service Improvement Team within 48 hours following the meeting.

Date: _____

Signatures of Service Improvement Team members:

_____   _____

_____   _____

_____   _____

_____   _____

_____   _____

Figure 3.6 (*Continued*)

The first thing we do at our meetings is read the minutes from our last meeting. If it only takes three minutes to describe it, why does it take three hours to do it?

Service Improvement Team meetings are not designed to be just another set of meetings in which talk occurs but no action results. The meetings focus on three areas: progress, plans, and challenges. Commitments are made and documented, input is received, communication takes place, and the members then get on with the work of executing the service improvement plan. The real work takes place outside of the meetings.

In those circumstances when we've seen Service Improvement Team meetings become unwieldy or unproductive, it's usually because members use the meetings to actually do the work of the initiative. Remember, the purpose of the Service Improvement Team meetings (after the initial organizational meetings) is to provide direction and communication and to ensure everything is moving ahead effectively—kind of like the way a board of directors would operate. Bogged-down Service Improvement Team meetings are usually an indicator that nothing is happening between meetings, which is when the action *should* be happening.

That being said, the first one or two meetings may feel messy and confusing. Everyone will be trying to get their arms around the service improvement effort and will have a lot of questions about the process. There may be more questions than answers. The development of a charter will help, but plan on some confusion and frustration; it's part of the teambuilding process. Developing the answers to questions together helps to unify the group. Figure 3.7 provides a sample agenda for the first meeting. We want to re-emphasize (and most of our clients would agree) that the first meeting is likely to be a bit chaotic. But follow the agenda, make commitments, and get things going while recognizing that you'll have to make adjustments along the way.

How Often to Meet/Length of Meetings

We've found that the first couple of Service Improvement Team meetings are long—a half day or sometimes even a full day. There's a lot of organizing and planning to be done at the initial meetings. Thereafter, 60 to 90 minutes is typical. An agenda is critical and it's important for the chairperson to keep things focused. Figure 3.8 provides a sample agenda for ongoing Service Improvement Team meetings.

We recommend that, at first, Service Improvement Team meetings be held every other week. After things are organized and under way, most groups meet once a month. That's enough time to get things done between meetings, while ensuring too much time doesn't pass without checking in with the whole

Service Improvement Team
First Meeting Agenda

I. Review purpose of the improvement effort and the role of the Service Improvement Team – Chairperson

    a. The purpose of the service improvement effort is to create a *sustainable* culture of service excellence throughout every facet of the organization

    b. The purpose of the Service Improvement Team is to ensure that each Leadership Action of the improvement effort is executed effectively and in concert with the other Leadership Actions

II. Review and sign the Service Improvement Team charter – Chairperson

    a. Questions or concerns regarding the charter

    b. Reinforcement of commitment required from each member of the team

    c. Signatures of the team

III. Schedule six months of Service Improvement Team meetings – Chairperson and Administrator

    a. Meetings should be a combination of face-to-face meetings and teleconferences. Face-to-face meetings, while inconvenient, will be most productive.

IV. Review sample Service Improvement Team commitment tracking sheet – Administrator

    a. Adapt as necessary

    b. Discuss distribution plan

V. Discuss initial Service Improvement Team activities – Entire team

    a. Strategy for development of the Service Philosophy and Standards (Chapter 4)

        1. Assign action steps

    b. Initial communications plan (Chapter 5)

        1. Assign action steps

VI. Develop plan for subteam – Entire team

    a. Selection criteria for subteam members

    b. Discussion of potential candidates

    c. Plan for contacting candidates

Figure 3.7 Sample Meeting Agenda (Go to www.UnleashingExcellence.com to download a customizable copy of this form.)

> **1.** Assign action steps
> **VII. Conclusion – Chairperson**
>   **a.** Review of commitments
>   **b.** Confirmation of next meeting

Figure 3.7 (*Continued*)

group. Take your own organization's situation into account. One client decided that because their operation is spread across three states they would meet face to face every other month and use conference calls for the other meetings.

Figure 3.9 shows a list of recommended ground rules to help keep your Service Improvement Team meetings focused and productive. We suggest you include the list with the agenda you send to your participants and post it in the meeting room,

---

Service Improvement Team
Ongoing Meeting Agenda
I. Welcome – Chairperson
  a. Review agenda
II. Service improvement initiative status check – Entire team
  a. Discussion of overall progress
  b. Success stories
III. Report out of each Leadership Action – Designated champions
  a. Progress made on action items
  b. Challenges encountered
  c. Next steps
IV. Conclusion – Chairperson
  a. Review of commitments – Administrator
  b. Confirmation of next meeting

Figure 3.8   Service Improvement Team Ongoing Meeting Agenda (Go to www.UnleashingExcellence.com to download a customizable copy of this form.)
Note: It's important to reinforce the linkages between each Leadership Action – each action is part of a cohesive whole. During the report outs, communication or coordination gaps may appear that need to be addressed.

Service Improvement Team Meeting Ground Rules

- Arrive prepared
- Arrive on time
- Notify chairperson if you are not able to attend and who will represent you
  - Notify chairperson if you know you will be arriving late
- Stay focused on the meeting topic
  - Mobile phones and Blackberries off
- Listen as an ally—build on ideas without criticizing
- Don't dominate the conversation
- Share your ideas and participate
  - Silence means consent
- One person speak at a time
- No side conversations
- After meeting is over, group speaks with one voice
- Follow through on commitments made

Figure 3.9   Recommended Ground Rules for Service Improvement Team Meetings (Go to www.UnleashingExcellence.com to download a customizable copy of this form.)

at least for the first few meetings. Referring back to these ground rules can keep the discussion from being sidetracked or derailed completely.

Subteams

We've referenced "subteams" several times in this chapter, and here we'll describe their role in the initiative.

The majority of the Service Improvement Team's work is actually done by a series of subteams, which are formed to execute the plans described in each chapter of this book. For example, the Communications subteam, led by the champion, puts together the communication plan, develops and implements the communication tools, keeps all communications fresh and up to date, along with the rest of the tactics described in Chapter 5.

How you structure your subteams will depend on your organizational structure, but here are some guidelines:

- Be sure to include frontline employees on each subteam. They provide valuable, real-world input and can also act as "ambassadors" for the initiative in their own work areas. Mark Yanarella, president of Naugatuck Savings Bank, said that one thing he wished they did differently at the beginning of their service initiative was to involve more frontline employees earlier in the process.
- Ensure that the subteams are cross functional. While it may not be possible to have every area of the company represented on a subteam, you want points of view from as many entities as possible. Ideally, each subteam should have no more than five to six members if they are to run efficiently.
- Follow the same meeting guidelines provided to the Service Improvement Team. Having an agenda, keeping track of commitments, and following up on accountabilities are all just as important with the subteams.
- Keep the members of the subteams excited and engaged. They need to know how their work fits into the overall initiative and what impact their work is having on the organization. The Service Improvement Team champions must be active liaisons between the Service Improvement Team and their subteams so that everyone knows how things are progressing with each Leadership Action as well as with the overall initiative.

In most cases, the subteams are fluid in their membership. A particular employee might be appropriate for the first activities of one of the Leadership Actions, but not for other activities. Or, after the initial work has been completed on a Leadership Action, some of the subteam members might join another subteam whose work is just beginning. Use your judgment as the initiative progresses regarding the best use of subteam members. You'll note that in the agenda for the first Service Improvement Team meeting, discussion of the subteams is included. A lively discussion is likely, as several Leadership Action champions all vie for certain "favorite" employees to be part of their team. There's no easy answer to this issue other than to make sure you spread the talent throughout the subteams.

Common Pitfalls of the Service Improvement Team

Anytime a group of people meets on a regular basis, there are bound to be some challenges. Here are some of the more common ones to guard against:

1. *The members of the Service Improvement Team are the only ones doing any work on the service improvement process.* A priority must be made of enlisting the help of employees throughout the organization on this entire effort. Get their input, involve them on subteams, and keep them informed. A Service Improvement Team that tries to do everything themselves is a recipe for burnout as well as employee disengagement.

2. *Meeting attendance starts to drop off.* The time commitment must be realistically discussed at the beginning of the initiative. It's idealistic to think that everyone will be able to attend every meeting. If, however, you notice that one or two members seem to miss a lot of meetings, ask them to re-evaluate their involvement on the team. There could be legitimate reasons for their continued absence, but it's wise to replace these individuals with members who can participate in the meetings.

3. *Meetings become bureaucratic nightmares.* If you see that the Service Improvement Team is not making decisions (dragging everything out), or is often deferring to other entities for approval, it may be a sign that the group doesn't have the necessary authority to get things done. Take another look at the make-up of the group. Or perhaps the group

needs to step back and readdress their charter, reaffirming the purpose of the group as a catalyst for *action*.

4. *The team is unwilling to take risks.* Part of the job of the Service Improvement Team is getting the organization out of its comfort zone. If you find that there are a lot of comments such as, "We've always done it that way," or "We've never done it that way," you can bet that creativity will eventually be stifled. Guard against complacency and encourage risk taking.

5. *Some members don't follow through on assignments.* The service improvement effort takes everyone's commitment. Someone who consistently drops the ball can bog down the whole process. It's possible that, once under way, a member proves to be ineffective as a part of the Service Improvement Team. He or she doesn't follow through on commitments, doesn't communicate effectively, or simply doesn't seem committed to the process. It's vital in such a circumstance that the chairperson step in and either counsel the member or find a replacement. While removing a member of the team is uncomfortable and unpleasant, it's important to the long-term success of the effort. One of the roles of the administrator is to follow up on Service Improvement Team member assignments. A lot of headaches can be eliminated with documentation and follow-up on assignments. We've all gotten that reminder phone call or e-mail that kept a task from accidentally falling through the cracks!

Special Situations

For organizations that are single-site locations, it's fairly easy to determine the make-up of the Service Improvement Team and to hold regular face-to-face meetings. It's more of a challenge to make up the Service Improvement Team in those organizations that have many dispersed or remote sites.

Here's how a bank comprised of a headquarters and 360 branches in three different states structured their Service Improvement Team: Leaders of the corporate entities and three regional managers make up a centralized team. They meet on a monthly basis, alternating face-to-face meetings with team conference calls to cut down on travel for those members in outlying areas. Each of the bank's regions has a "regional implementation team," which carries out the plans developed by the corporate team. The regional implementation teams are made up of employees from individual branches who have shown enthusiasm and concern for service excellence. These employees are also informal leaders among their peers within the branches. The bank's regional implementation teams not only carry out the implementation plans, but they also tailor the plans when necessary to fit the culture of the region. Constant communication keeps everything working.

Adapt the structure so it works for your situation. Nothing is carved in stone.

Ongoing Service Improvement Teams

One of the qualities that makes this process different from the usual flavor-of-the-month program is the turning over of the Service Improvement Team after a period of time to a new group of members. It's a never-ending process. The work of the first Service Improvement Team is to design the initial plans, educate all associates on the initiative, and put key systems in place. The role of the second and subsequent Service Improvement Teams is to refine and enhance the systems, provide refresher training, and continue heightening the awareness of service excellence. New ideas, fresh enthusiasm, and different perspectives are brought in by new team members.

We recommend that you not turn over the whole team each year, but instead keep half of the members to provide continuity and a historical perspective. Half the group rotates off the team

yearly. Train all new members on the entire process and specifically on their roles and responsibilities. Hold a celebration to
acknowledge the outgoing members and introduce the new
members of the team. It's an excellent way to communicate to
the rest of the organization that the service improvement process
is alive and ongoing. One client highlighted this changing of the
guard by actually holding a ceremony with the outgoing members
literally passing a baton to the new Service Improvement Team
members.

Concluding Thoughts

Whew! This was a tough chapter. Some organizations complain,
"Not another committee!" We agree organizations often have
too many committees and meetings. The Service Improvement
Team, however, is a cornerstone of this effort. Without such a
group acting as a rudder for the effort, lasting success will be
difficult to attain. There is simply too much to be done to make it
all work without a dedicated, energized team to guide the effort
along. So, yes, we suppose the Service Improvement Team could
be viewed as another committee. We're confident, however, that
it has the potential to be the most important committee in the
organization. After all, the team's focus is the customer—who
ultimately supports the organization and ensures everyone's job.

Service Improvement Team Action Steps

- Choose the Service Improvement Team members, selecting
  8 to 10 members at the most.
- Ensure that the team represents a cross section of the
  organization.
- Have as many senior-level members as possible on the first
  Service Improvement Team. They need to have the authority to get things done.

- Select a Service Improvement Team administrator.
- Draft a team charter and create a meeting schedule.
- Assign a Leadership Action to individual team members based on their skills, talents, and expertise.
- Announce the formation, purpose, and membership of the Service Improvement Team to the rest of the organization.
- Create cross functional subteams for each Leadership Action.
- Keep meetings between 60 to 90 minutes. Run the meetings efficiently.
- Adapt the process to fit your organization's unique needs.
- Begin rotating in new members approximately 12 months into the initiative.

Pitfalls to Avoid

- Don't allow the Service Improvement Team to become the Service Improvement Police.
- Don't set organization-wide expectations that the Service Improvement Team will be doing all of the work on the improvement effort.
- Don't be disappointed if the first couple of Service Improvement Team meetings are confusing or frustrating. It's part of the teambuilding process.
- Don't allow noncommitted members to reduce the effectiveness of the Service Improvement Team. Changes may be necessary.
- Don't get bogged down in bureaucracy. Make decisions!

Chapter Four

DEVELOPING THE SERVICE IMPROVEMENT CORE TOOLS

"Our company decided that customer service was going to be a priority for every department and every employee. There was a big rally with banners and music to get everyone excited. It kind of worked; everything they said in the meeting made sense. Who would argue that customer service isn't important, right? Most of us left the meeting pretty charged up. The main problem was that there was no consistency about what great service *is*. We all had our own opinions of how things should be done. Some departments did great stuff. Some departments didn't do anything. We were just making it up as we went along. After a while, we got tired of making it up. We still get the same customer complaints we've always gotten."

Changing employee behaviors is one of the most daunting challenges of any service initiative. Without guidance, every employee has his or her own image of what service is and how it should or should not be delivered. Visit nearly any store or restaurant and you'll see as many varieties of service as there are employees. One employee is smiling, friendly, and efficient, while another is distant and apathetic. Which employee ends up serving you is often the luck of the draw. Who hasn't had the experience of getting in the "wrong" line at the supermarket? Other shoppers happily zoom through the line right next to yours, parting with a friendly wave from the checkout clerk. You stand there boiling as your checkout clerk struggles with the scanner and carries a facial expression that announces that life in general is rotten.

Clearly, there are bad employees out there. You could probably name employees in your organization who have no business working there. Often, however, the problem lies in the fact that management has not communicated the organization's service "nonnegotiables." These are behaviors that define your organization's identity. Violation of these nonnegotiables, even once, diminishes that identity.

In Chapter 1 we introduced several concepts that make up the foundation of the service improvement approach we recommend:

- See everything through the *lens of the customer.*
- Pay attention to the physical environment because *everything speaks.*
- Provide service delivery that will *create service wows.*
- Develop processes that make employees *service heroes.*

In this chapter we're going to describe some of the tools that help to "inculturate" these concepts. The champion and subteam of this Leadership Action are responsible for developing the tools and for ensuring that they are incorporated into each of the other Leadership Actions. While there are certainly other tools that will be introduced throughout this book, these are the core tools that drive everything else.

Anytime you want to know how things are going from a service perspective, just see if the organization is using the core tools. Anytime you want to coach an employee on his or her customer service skills, the core tools can provide a foundation for the discussion. They answer the question: "What's expected of me?"

Core Tool #1: The Service Philosophy

Most organizations today have a mission statement. Many organizations also have a vision statement, a purpose statement, a statement regarding statements, and so on. It becomes mind-boggling as teams creating these statements try to include everything the company does, ever has done, and ever hopes to do. One company we know of has a mission statement that is two pages long, containing language that was word-smithed into meaninglessness. No one in the company, including the executive team, can verbalize what's contained in the statement. We've all been there when a new company mission or vision statement is rolled out. Usually a wallet card is given as a magical device to help everyone remember the mission statement. Two weeks later, ask someone to recite it. You're usually met with a blank stare as the employee fumbles to find the wallet card (which he or she probably doesn't have).

Our purpose here is not to belittle the value of mission and vision statements. A clear mission and vision helps leaders make strategic decisions that affect the company's future. The fallacy, however, is in believing that these statements impact the behavior of rank and file employees. They don't. Most of our employees are in the trenches, dealing with a never-ending stream of customers, returning phone calls, trying to make a sale, and fighting to stay ahead of the volume of work to be done and still make it to their child's school play. Expecting employees to constantly think in terms of value-added, market leadership, and "world's foremost" is simply unrealistic. There needs to be something that is truly meaningful to an employee's day-to-day job that provides direction as well as inspiration. This is the purpose of the Service Philosophy.

The Service Philosophy defines your true product or service— what the customer is *really* buying from your organization. (Remember the old sales expression: The customer doesn't need a ½ inch drill bit; the customer needs a ½ inch hole.) Most importantly, the Service Philosophy answers the question: how should I as an employee serve our customers? A few examples will help illustrate what we mean. Here are examples of what we would call Service Philosophies:

> Walt Disney World: *"We create happiness by providing the finest in entertainment for people of all ages, everywhere."*
>
> Community Blood Center of the Ozarks: *"We enrich lives in our community by working together to create trust and confidence in all we do."*
>
> First Citizens Bank: *"We build life-enhancing relationships by helping our customers identify and achieve their financial goals."*
>
> Westgate Resorts: *"We fulfill our guests' dreams by providing a vacation experience that exceeds all expectations."*
>
> Seminole Community College: *"We change lives by empowering, inspiring and educating our students and the community."*
>
> Cool Cuts 4 Kids: *"We create excitement by engaging our customers in a fun, friendly, family experience."*

You can see from these examples that each organization's beliefs about customer service are clearly communicated to the employee.

What is the "true product" of the organization?

- Walt Disney World—Happiness
- Community Blood Center of the Ozarks—Enriched lives
- First Citizens Bank—Life-enhancing relationships
- Westgate Resorts—Fulfilled vacation dreams
- Seminole Community College—Changed lives
- Cool Cuts 4 Kids—Excitement

How should I serve our customers?

- Walt Disney World—Create happiness
- Community Blood Center of the Ozarks—Enrich lives
- First Citizens Bank—Build life-enhancing relationships

- Westgate Resorts—Fulfill guests' vacation dreams
- Seminole Community College—Change lives
- Cool Cuts 4 Kids—Create excitement

Is this approach overly simple? Simple—yes; Overly—no. In each of the previous cases, it's easy for every employee in the organization to keep the Service Philosophy top of mind. Each example is easy to explain, train, and coach. Each one clearly identifies the company's position on service. What more could you ask for from a statement?

If you've ever taken a photograph of your family at Walt Disney World, it's likely that a cast member offered to take the picture for you. The whole family is able to be in the picture. Why did the cast member do that? Because her job is to "create happiness." Her tasks may be to sweep streets, serve ice cream cones, sell balloons, or whatever. But her job is to create happiness. And 55,000 Walt Disney World cast members do exactly that.

Keep in mind that statements such as those noted above are not magical—we're not kidding ourselves. There must be support systems that allow employees to deliver on the Service Philosophy. But clear direction is the starting point.

What About Support Staff?

Chances are that many of your employees don't directly interact with customers. The question becomes: Does the Service Philosophy apply to support employees? They have internal customers and this approach doesn't seem to fit. It fits. There is a running debate about internal and external customers. Make no mistake about it—internal and external customer service go hand-in-hand. Everyone in the organization has customers. Often these customers are other employees somewhere in the company. If these internal customers don't receive great service, it is unlikely that they will be able (or willing) to provide great service to external customers.

"I was working on a report that I had to present to a customer later that day. I was trying to import some data from another document and I must've done something the computer didn't like, because it froze up. I tried everything, but it wouldn't unfreeze. I finally called our Information Services department and they sent over a technician to fix it. The guy made me feel like an idiot. I know I probably caused the problem, but there's no excuse for the way he treated me. I'm supposed to be his customer! I tried not to let it get to me, but he definitely put me in a bad mood."

It's a rare organization that can have poor internal service while delivering great external service. Every division, every department, and every employee must understand how their jobs impact the ultimate, revenue-generating customer. If someone states, "This service philosophy doesn't apply to my group because we are so far removed from the ultimate customer," we would question the need for that group's existence. If they don't impact the final customer, why does the function exist? By the way, simply make this observation and watch how fast the group's connection to the customer is made. Service excellence must be an organization-wide priority if the effort is to be successful.

Developing the Service Philosophy

The Service Philosophy answers two questions:

1. What do we do?
2. How do we do it?

What do we do?	How do we do it?
"We create happiness."	"By providing the finest in entertainment for people of all ages, everywhere."
"We enrich lives."	"By working together to create trust and confidence in all we do."

"We build life-enhancing relationships."	"By helping our customers identify and achieve their financial goals."
"We fulfill our guests' dreams."	"By providing a vacation experience that exceeds all expectations."
"We change lives."	"By empowering, inspiring and educating our students and community."
"We create excitement."	"By engaging our customers in a fun, friendly, family experience."

We've found that the best approach to developing a Service Philosophy is to put together a cross functional group of employees, from all levels of the organization, for a facilitated one-day workshop. The first part of the workshop clearly outlines the objective and purpose of a Service Philosophy. The rest of the session is devoted to brainstorming the answers to customer-related issues and using the responses to then craft the Service Philosophy.

Breaking the development team into small groups and having each group come up with their own ideas and then bring these ideas back to the large group works well. It allows you to cut and paste between the group's ideas to come up with a short, simple statement that everyone likes and agrees to. Figure 4.1 provides a worksheet that can be used for brainstorming purposes.

We'll warn you that it's hard to keep people from focusing on the tangible product or service or from going to the trite and boring response of "we're selling customer satisfaction." The Service Philosophy must be inspiring—something that motivates the employee beyond the mechanical tasks of his or her job.

We'll also warn you that the dynamics of the brainstorming session can get intense, and sometimes mind-numbing, as *every word* of the Service Philosophy is debated, revised, and re-ordered. The frustration is worth it, however, because the team is forced to wrestle with what the organization really provides to customers. Just remember to keep the Service Philosophy simple and ensure it answers the two questions: What do we do? and, How do we do it?

The Service Philosophy

A Service Philosophy is a brief, motivating statement that clearly defines what customers should experience during any encounter with your organization. It explains what you do, and how you do it. What is the Service Philosophy for your organization? What do you want your employees to focus on as they interact with customers? In other words, what do you want your employees to "create"?

1. **At the conclusion of any interaction with our organization, what words or phrases describe the emotions our customers should feel?**

   _____
   _____
   _____
   _____

2. **How do we want customers to describe our organization to others?**

   _____
   _____
   _____
   _____

3. **With the responses to questions 1 & 2 in mind, what should be the Service Philosophy of our organization?**

   _____
   _____
   _____
   _____

Figure 4.1   The Service Philosophy (Go to www.UnleashingExcellence .com to download a customizable copy of this form.)

Testing the Service Philosophy

You may want to test the Service Philosophy on several employees to get their reactions before communicating it to the entire organization. A word of warning: Don't expect any of the test subjects, upon reading the statement, to fall on their knees and proclaim that you've just changed their lives. It's not going to happen. More than likely you will get responses such as, "What is this for again?" and "Is someone actually getting paid for producing this?" Simply try to get the person talking. Discussion-generating questions might include: "How well does this philosophy fit your job?" "How would you change the statement?" "If a new hire were to read this, would it accurately describe what our company does?" You are simply looking for nuggets of information that may help refine the Service Philosophy as well as illustrations that will help explain it.

Core Tool #2: The Service Standards

In his book *Good to Great,* Jim Collins says: "A culture of discipline involves a duality. On the one hand, it requires people who adhere to a consistent system; yet, on the other hand, it gives people freedom and responsibility within the framework of that system." Consistent Service Standards help provide such a framework.

The good news is that the Service Standards are developed at the same time you develop the Service Philosophy. Same process, same input. The purpose of the Service Standards, however, is different than that of the Service Philosophy. While the Service Philosophy describes the organization's true product, the Service Standards describe the behaviors needed to deliver the true product.

Imagine telling 5,000 bank employees, "Go build life-enhancing relationships with our customers," providing no other guidance. There are many ways to build life-enhancing relationships, some of which may not be appropriate for a bank. There must be behavioral guidelines that provide direction on *how* employees are expected to build these life-enhancing relationships. Providing that guidance is the role of the Service Standards.

The Difference Between Service Standards and Company Values

We have yet to run into a company of any size that does not have written company values. We also have yet to run into a company whose written values are not 95 percent identical to the values of every other organization. Most would include integrity, teamwork, customer focus, respect for diversity, innovation, and so on. We concede that company values are important. If the values are enforced, they can provide a moral compass for the organization. If the values are not enforced, they are meaningless.

Service Standards are different. They are the "rules of engagement" for providing customer service. Service Standards provide the behavioral template that leads to consistent service. They help employees at the moment of truth—those times they have to make a service decision. Again, a few examples will help illustrate what we mean. Walt Disney World has their well-publicized standards of:

1. Safety
2. Courtesy
3. Show (attention to detail)
4. Efficiency

Their standards are in prioritized order. Safety is never compromised for any reason. Courtesy will never be sacrificed for the sake of the show. For example, someone wearing a futuristic Tomorrowland uniform (costume) would never pass through turn-of-the-century Main Street, USA (with its early 1900s theme) on his way to take a break. This action would detract from the show (Disney calls it a "visual intrusion"). If, however, that same

Blood Bank	Resort Hotel
1. Safety	1. Responsive
2. Accuracy	2. Accurate
3. Respectfulness	3. Helpful
4. Efficiency	4. Informative
Bank	**Hospital**
1. Accuracy	1. Safety
2. Responsive	2. Respect/Dignity
3. Courtesy	3. Efficiency
4. Partnership	

Figure 4.2   Examples of Service Standards

cast member noticed a guest in need of directions or help, who happened to be on Main Street, USA, the cast member is fully empowered to assist the guest even though there is a "violation" of the show standard. Why is this violation acceptable? Because courtesy is a higher priority than show. See how it works?

Figure 4.2 provides several examples of Service Standards clients have developed.

The majority of the time, all of the Service Standards are working together with no need to worry about their hierarchy. The moment the employee needs to make a service decision, however, the hierarchy of standards becomes critical. For instance, as an employee working in the bank example in Figure 4.2, I am encouraged to get an answer to a request back quickly for a customer. If, however, I am not sure of the answer, is it better to respond with what I *think* or *know for certain* is the answer? I should *know for certain* what the answer is, because accuracy takes priority over responsiveness. It would be better, even if it took a little more time, to make certain I have the correct answer for the customer. The Service Standards provide employees with guidance in making effective service decisions. Later in the chapter we'll describe the process for prioritizing the Service Standards.

Again, What About Support Staff?

Let's revisit the dilemma about applying a customer service tool to the support staff. Yes, the same Service Standards apply to support staff. No, the words shouldn't be tweaked to fit better. If any tweaking needs to be done, do it in the explaining and training processes; don't change the words. Keeping the Service Standards consistent is critical.

Look at the Walt Disney World standards: safety, courtesy, show, and efficiency. Let's observe how the standards apply to a "backstage" cast member who is responsible for painting the ornate wooden (or fiberglass) horses on Cinderella's Carousel. If you have ever seen these beautiful carousel horses, then you've experienced the work of these talented craftspeople. Clearly, the standard these cast members spend most of their time focused on is "show." They are making these horses beautiful for the guests. Efficiency also gets a lot of attention, since there is a production schedule to be met. So the order of the standards changes, right? You know by now that it doesn't. Time spent has nothing to do with the prioritized order. If the painter discovers a safety issue, such as a crack in the shell of one of the horses, all other bets are off. Fixing the safety problem becomes job one. What about courtesy? If this cast member should interact with a guest, courtesy is in its proper place in the hierarchy. Let's imagine that the painter is "onstage" checking out the quality of the carousel, and a guest asks a question. The painter is expected to be courteous and provide or find the answer. Do situations like this happen a lot? Probably not, but the painter knows her responsibility when a situation does occur.

Developing the Service Standards

As we mentioned earlier in the chapter, the Service Standards are developed at the same time you are developing the Service Philosophy. Use some of the Service Standard examples provided earlier as guidelines on the type of words used in effective Service Standards. First, look for the no-brainers. In healthcare, for example, something like accuracy or safety better be pretty close to the top of the hierarchy. If the doctor or nurse isn't accurate, nothing else really counts. Imagine a friendly nurse who has to jab you six times to hit a vein when drawing blood. The friendliness is nice, but, given the choice, wouldn't you rather have her get it right the first time?

An additional mindset for developing appropriate Service Standards is to consider what behaviors or oversights irritate customers and then brainstorm standards that might prevent those situations from happening. For example, if you hear comments like the following, you may get clues as to what standards would be important to your customers.

"I can never get anyone on the phone."
"No one returns my calls."
"One department doesn't seem to know what the other is doing."
"Your employees seem rushed."
"Some of your people are nice and some are unfriendly."
"No one is able to answer my questions."
"Your employees seem to be more interested in talking with each other than helping customers."

Our recommendation is that your final list be comprised of three to five standards. More than five become unwieldy in practice. With that number in mind, it's time to begin narrowing your long list. Figure 4.3 provides some guidelines for developing your list.

Prioritizing the Service Standards

Now that you have a narrowed list of standards, it's time to prioritize them. Without prioritization, 4 standards have 24 possible variations. That level of variation provides no real guidance for your employees. As you review the standards you've developed, which one is most important? Now, of the standards remaining, which is most important? Once you have a rough

- **Each standard on the final list should be unique from every other standard.**

  For example, accuracy and precision are too close in meaning to be separate standards. Courtesy and friendliness are too close. Similar standards don't help employees make service decisions. This principle is important! Following this principle now will save you untold headaches later on.

- **Each standard should be actionable.**

  Look again at the examples provided earlier. It's easy to put actions to the words. Employees easily understand what the words mean.

- **The standards must focus on customer service.**

  You will be tempted, for example, to use *teamwork* as a service standard. This magical word tempts everyone. Teamwork is not a service standard. Teamwork is an important internal process or value for achieving results, but it's not a customer service standard. Try putting Teamwork in the Disney standards and see if it helps make a service decision. It doesn't.

Figure 4.3   Guidelines for Developing Service Standards

prioritization, test out your Service Standards on various situations that might occur in your organization. Does the order make sense? You'll probably move things around a bit as you work through this exercise, and you may find yourself frustrated. Frustration is okay because you are forcing yourself to validate all of your hard work. Review the service standard examples earlier in the chapter and note the logic behind the prioritization.

Defining the Service Standards

Once you have prioritized the Service Standards, the next step is to define them so everyone knows exactly what is expected and included in each behavior. Figure 4.4 shows how one organization defined their Service Standards to make it very clear to all employees what was expected. Note how each Service Standard contains a descriptor of what the standard means, followed by several bullet

- **Dependability**—We "do the job right." We perform with precision and ensure error-free interactions with each customer.
  - Maintain the absolute privacy/confidentiality of the customer transaction.
  - Pay attention to every detail of the transaction.
  - Know all bank products or where to obtain correct information.
  - Listen carefully to ensure true understanding of the customer's need.
  - Ensure the customer's understanding of the transaction.

- **Accessibility**—We are easy to do business with. We are consistently available and responsive to our customers and always ensure that their experience with us is efficient and timely.
  - Acknowledge the customer promptly.
  - Conduct each transaction efficiently.
  - Keep all commitments/return calls promptly.

- **Collaboration**—We care about the long-term success of each customer and strive to build trust-based, collaborative relationships.
  - Treat customers as welcome guests.
  - Learn and use customers' names.
  - Look at each transaction as an opportunity to build trust with the customer.
  - Focus on building customer partnerships that are life-long and strong enough to pass to the next generation.

- **Advice**—Our customers learn from us and are better because of the relationship.
  - Inform customers of new, beneficial products that provide solutions to their needs.
  - Constantly learn about customers and help them to identify their needs.
  - Always be on the lookout for ways to further assist each customer.

Figure 4.4   Service Standards—Example

points that provide examples of behaviors that demonstrate the standard in action. Each area of the organization should expand on the list to include behaviors specific to that area.

Core Tool #3: Service Mapping

In Chapter 1 we discussed the importance of looking at your operation through the *lens of the customer.* Service Mapping is a tool that not only reinforces the lens of the customer mindset; it is also a tool for making organizational processes more customer-friendly. This section will describe the process for creating a Service Map, but keep in mind it is not a one-time event. It should be used on an ongoing basis by every area of the organization in order to continually improve processes.

The first step in Service Mapping is to identify a process you would like to improve in order to improve the customer experience. You might decide to focus on a broad process, such as "the overall shopping experience in our store," or a segment of the process, such as "the checkout process in our store." It depends on the organization and where the improvement opportunities exist.

After deciding on a process on which to focus, put together a team made up of employees involved in the process and conduct a Service Mapping session.

Conducting a Service Mapping Session

There should be a facilitator for the session. The facilitator might be a member of the Service Improvement Team subcommittee, the leader of the department, an outside facilitator, or a member of the department trained in using the tool.

The first step is to map the process using the template shown in Figure 4.5. Please note that most of your processes will likely be more than nine steps; Figure 4.5 is simply provided as an example. Using a flipchart or whiteboard, the team maps out the process *through the lens of the customer.* Each step must begin with "The customer . . . " For example, if someone in the group says

Process Analyzed:_____

Step 1: Describe each step of the process through the "lens of the customer."

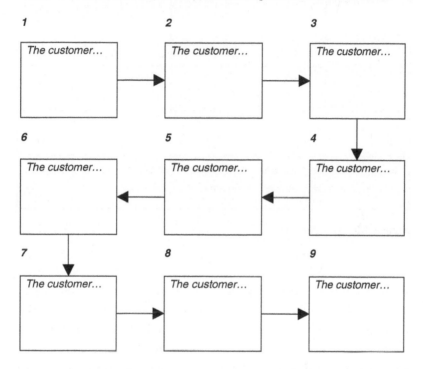

Step 2: For each block identified in step 1, describe what would be considered mediocre service and what would be considered excellent service.

Block Number	Mediocre Service	Excellent Service

Figure 4.5   Service Map—Template (Go to www.UnleashingExcellence .com to download a customizable copy of this form.)

Block Number	Mediocre Service	Excellent Service

Step 3: Choose one or two of the steps to focus on improving first, then move on to other steps that are determined to be areas of opportunity.

Figure 4.5 (*Continued*)

something like, "Next we process the paperwork," the facilitator should ask, "While we're processing the paperwork, what's the customer doing?" The answer in this case is that the customer is *waiting* while the paperwork is processed. Now you have something to work with since the step is now seen through the lens of the customer.

After completing the Service Map and ensuring that each step is described from the customer's perspective, the next step is to look at each component of the Service Map and ask, "What would mediocre service look like at this step?" The reason it's important to define mediocre service is that in many cases, after describing mediocre, it becomes apparent that at some of the steps the service currently delivered is indeed mediocre. Remember, we're not talking about *poor* service; we're talking about mediocre, transaction-like service. What we've found in conducting countless Service Mapping sessions with clients is that, while they may be providing excellent service at some of the steps, they're now looking at the *entire* experience and can usually see that there are many opportunities throughout the experience for improvement.

After describing mediocre service, the next step is to describe excellent service at each step. A word of caution here. When team members are brainstorming what excellent service would look like, don't let the words, ''We can't do that, because . . . '' creep into the conversation. The purpose of the discussion is to describe excellent service, and you don't want to censure yourselves at this point. You may not be able to implement every idea presented, but it's better to set your sights high and get as close to the ideal as possible than to stifle conversation early and only generate ideas that are slightly above mediocre.

The final step of the Service Mapping session is to take the descriptions of excellence and re-map the experience using these descriptions. Figure 4.6 shows an example of a completed

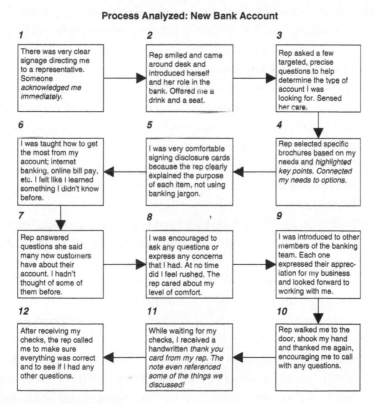

Process Analyzed: New Bank Account

1 There was very clear signage directing me to a representative. Someone *acknowledged me immediately.*

2 Rep smiled and came around desk and introduced herself and her role in the bank. Offered me a drink and a seat.

3 Rep asked a few targeted, precise questions to help determine the type of account I was looking for. Sensed her care.

6 I was taught how to get the most from my account; internet banking, online bill pay, etc. I felt like I learned something I didn't know before.

5 I was very comfortable signing disclosure cards because the rep clearly explained the purpose of each item, not using banking jargon.

4 Rep selected specific brochures based on my needs and *highlighted key points. Connected my needs to options.*

7 Rep answered questions she said many new customers have about their account. I hadn't thought of some of them before.

8 I was encouraged to ask any questions or express any concerns that I had. At no time did I feel rushed. The rep cared about my level of comfort.

9 I was introduced to other members of the banking team. Each one expressed their appreciation for my business and looked forward to working with me.

12 After receiving my checks, the rep called me to make sure everything was correct and to see if I had any other questions.

11 While waiting for my checks, I received a handwritten *thank you* card from my rep. The note even referenced some of the things we discussed!

10 Rep walked me to the door, shook my hand and thanked me again, encouraging me to call with any questions.

Figure 4.6   Service Map

Service Map for opening a checking account. As you can see, each step describes how excellent service should be delivered from the perspective of the customer.

Service Mapping Outcomes

Clients who've consistently used Service Mapping have reported outstanding results in improving the customer experience. Some of the improvements have required investment of money; others have simply required behavioral changes.

Cummins Southern Plains Service Mapped their process for repairing diesel truck engines, looking at the process through the lens of the truck operator. Their philosophy is that when someone buys a Cummins product, "they bought us." They recognize that people make a living with their product. Based on input from the distributorship team, they enhanced the experience in several ways:

- They updated the drivers' lounges at the branches to increase the comfort of the operators as they wait for the repair, including internet access and discounts for local restaurants and hotels. And they don't just leave the driver sitting there; they keep them informed of the progress of the repair.
- Team members transport truck operators to local malls and restaurants if requested, so that they don't have to sit in the lounge the entire time.
- Rather than simply handing the keys to the operator following a service event and sending the operator to search the lot for the truck, a technician or service advisor now brings the truck around to the operator, reviews the repairs, describes any items the operator should keep an eye on, and thanks them for their business. They also provide the operator with the contact information of Cummins' distributorships around the country in the event a problem occurs on the road. The Service Manager offers his or her business card just in case the operator needs to make contact for any reason.

Georgia Southern University knows that college life can be overwhelming, especially for new students. They Service Mapped several processes in order to make the experience less stressful and more rewarding for their customers—their students.

- The staff recognized that, while university life can be stressful for any student, it can be especially stressful for students from other cultures. Previously, students responding to a flyer about the university's multicultural resources were simply provided with written information when visiting the multicultural office. Now, the students meet with a member of the professional staff to ensure all questions are answered, and they are then invited to give input for future programs to help make the transition easier.
- Just as the beginning of a student's college time can be stressful, so can preparing for graduation. Not only do they need to make plans for the next phase of their lives, they need to make sure they've completed the graduation requirements! The university has streamlined the process by proactively sending notifications to potential graduates on their "MyGeorgiaSouthern" intranet account, letting them know, "It's time to apply." They also manage the students' expectations by carefully describing the process and filling out a degree evaluation before seeing an advisor, ensuring that the advisor has enough information to accurately guide students through the process.

The staff of Springfield Clinic in Springfield, Illinois, knows that any healthcare issue generates a lot of stress for patients, especially when the issue is an emergency. And long wait times tend to magnify the stress. So, Springfield Clinic's Prompt Care department got together as a team over a series of meetings and Service Mapped the entire Prompt Care visit. The Springfield Clinic Prompt Care department chairperson emphasizes that team participation has been the key to their success. The team's efforts have resulted in patient satisfaction scores amongst the highest in all of Springfield Clinic and a reduction in wait time from 1–2 hours to an average of 20 minutes. Some of the actions they took to achieve these results include the following:

- Rather than waiting for the lab to pick up tests, Prompt Care team members take any tests that don't require a blood draw to the lab with the agreement that the lab will turn the test around on the spot; And for those tests that do require a blood draw, lab personnel now come to the patient in Prompt Care rather than sending the patient to the lab.
- Two additional providers were added to the Prompt Care team in order to reduce the wait as well as increase the amount of time team members can spend with patients (a key driver of patient satisfaction).
- As a team, they developed specific expectations for nurse-patient interactions using the book *Love Your Patients!* by Scott Louis Diering as a source of healthcare-specific behaviors that lead to patient satisfaction.

Putting Service Mapping to Use

Once a Service Map has been completed, it's important that all appropriate employees are trained on the behaviors defined on the Service Map and that everyone is held accountable for those behaviors. The Service Map is also used to train new employees—"Here's how we differentiate ourselves in this process from other organizations."

Service Mapping is an ongoing process. The organization as well as individual teams continually move on to other processes as each is inculturated, resulting in ongoing service improvement.

Core Tool #4: The Everything Speaks Checklist

Chapter 1 introduced the concept of *everything speaks*, meaning that every detail of an organization's physical environment communicates a message to customers. The question is, what message is your organization's physical environment communicating?

The Everything Speaks Checklist is a tool that transforms *everything speaks* from being merely a philosophy to being an organization-wide practice. Figure 4.7 is an example of an Everything Speaks Checklist developed for a hospital entrance. At an assigned time, a member of the team walks the facility, checklist in hand, checking each item on the list. Anything checked as unsatisfactory is either handled on the spot or called in to the appropriate department to handle the problem.

The example in Figure 4.7 is simply a template that will need to be adapted to your own organization. A small health clinic, for example, might have a single checklist that encompasses the entire facility. A large hospital might have multiple checklists covering various departments or units. Customize the Everything Speaks Checklist so it makes sense for your organization.

Regardless of how you structure your organization's Everything Speaks Checklist, here are a few suggestions for getting the most from the tool:

- Put together a team (or several teams) to create the checklist(s). Having employees involved in creating the checklists increases buy-in and gets members of the team focusing on the details of the physical environment.
- Train all team members on the Everything Speaks Checklist—its use as well as its purpose. As you walk the area during the training, define what qualifies as Satisfactory and Unsatisfactory.
- The Everything Speaks Checklist should be completed *every* day. Doing the checklist every day dramatically accelerates inculturation of the everything speaks philosophy. Doing it every day also brings a level of accountability to the process that isn't possible when done infrequently.
- Responsibility for completing the checklist should be rotated amongst all staff members, including each member of

Everything Speaks Checklist

Area: Hospital Entrance/Admitting

Date:_____

Conducted by:_____

Parking/Outside Entrance

Item	Satisfactory	Unsatisfactory	Action
Signage			
Parking Lot Condition			
Landscape Condition			
Overall Cleanliness			
Lighting Fixtures			

Additional Comments:_____
_____
_____

Lobby Area

Item	Satisfactory	Unsatisfactory	Action
Cleanliness			
Lighting			
Furniture Condition			
Signage			
Window Cleanliness			
Displays, Brochures, etc. Stocked, Clean			
Overall Condition			

Additional Comments:_____
_____
_____

Figure 4.7 Everything Speaks Checklist (Go to www.UnleashingExcellence .com to download a customizable copy of this form.)

Admitting Area

Item	Satisfactory	Unsatisfactory	Action
Free of Clutter			
Supplies (Forms, Pens, Cards, etc.)			
Lighting			
Appropriate Seating Available			
Condition of Furniture			
Overall Maintenance			
Confidential Information Out of View (Files, etc.)			

Additional Comments:_____

_____

_____

Restrooms

Item	Satisfactory	Unsatisfactory	Action
Supplies			
Overall Cleanliness			
Lighting			
Overall Maintenance			

Additional Comments:_____

_____

_____

Figure 4.7 (*Continued*)

the management team. Such a rotation demonstrates that everyone is responsible for the environment and helps everyone develop an eye for detail. Again, a large physical environment will require checklists for individual areas, completed by those responsible for the appropriate area. Once up and running, a checklist should take no longer than 15 minutes to complete.

- Any item checked as unsatisfactory must have an action noted in the appropriate section of the form.
- Completed checklists should be reviewed regularly for any trends that may appear. One client, for example, changed landscaping companies because of consistent unsatisfactory ratings on landscape quality. The new landscape company knows that their work is checked *every day*.

Many of our consulting clients have told us that the Everything Speaks Checklist has been a catalyst of the entire service improvement initiative due to its highly visible impact and company-wide employee involvement.

The Role of the Service Improvement Team

Each of the tools described in this chapter—the Service Philosophy, the Service Standards, Service Mapping, and the Everything Speaks Checklist—must be created, distributed, and managed. The Everything Speaks Checklist, for example, could be easily introduced to the organization and then never used. The champion and subteam for the Service Improvement Core Tools Leadership Action are responsible not only for ensuring that each entity of the organization develops its checklist, but also for conducting spot checks to make sure the checklist is being used, trends are tracked, and ongoing problems are addressed. The champion and subteam are responsible for working with the Accountability Leadership Action champion in ensuring that the Service Standards are incorporated into job descriptions, performance appraisals, and other accountability tools.

Texas Bank and Trust, based in Longview, Texas, came up with a fun way to encourage all employees to remember the bank's Service Standards. Every employee was given a specially engraved coin with their standards: Secure, Accurate, Responsive, and Courteous. Any employee can throw down their coin in front of any other employee (including senior management) and challenge them to recite the Service Philosophy and Service Standards. The team has fun with the game and, more importantly, it encourages everyone to know the Service Philosophy and Service Standards. One of the bank's tellers even challenged the Chairman with the game. And, yes, the Chairman successfully responded.

With constant reinforcement, the Service Improvement Core Tools will become part of the organizational culture and will literally transform the customer experience. The champion and subteam for this Leadership Action ensure that the tools are developed, understood, and used.

Concluding Thoughts

Through the rest of the book, you'll see how the Service Improvement Core Tools weave through the Unleashing Excellence approach. In Chapter 5 we'll discuss getting word out about the service improvement initiative and how these tools support the process. In Chapter 6 we'll describe the various training programs that introduce the details of the service improvement initiative and begin training all employees on the use of the tools. In fact, each of the Leadership Actions described in the chapters that follow are designed to inculturate service excellence behaviors, and the tools described in this chapter will play a key role in the process.

Service Improvement Team Action Steps

- Select a cross functional, multilevel group to participate in a one-day workshop for developing the organization's Service Philosophy and Service Standards.
- Develop the Service Philosophy; keep it short and simple.
- Make sure the Service Philosophy addresses the two questions: *What do we do?* and *How do we do it?*
- Keep the Service Standards behaviorally oriented.
- Prioritize the Service Standards.
- Test the Service Philosophy and Standards with cross levels of employees to ensure understanding and validity.
- Develop sample Service Maps and Everything Speaks Checklists to be used in the training programs described in Chapter 6.
- Ensure that the Service Improvement Core Tools are included in the activities of each Leadership Action.
- Conduct regular spot checks to ensure that Service Mapping and Everything Speaks Checklists are being used throughout the organization.

Pitfalls to Avoid

- Don't let the Service Philosophy be written as a general, watered-down statement with little or no meaning.
- Don't allow one person to develop the Service Philosophy and Standards; it should be a group effort.
- Don't develop two sets of standards—one for frontline employees and one for support.
- Don't allow the Service Standards to change depending upon situations or timing.
- Don't let using the Service Improvement Core Tools simply become an exercise; they should be used to guide decisions and solve real issues.

Chapter Five

COMMUNICATION

A heart-warming ritual took place during the construction of a new building at the Dana-Farber Cancer Institute in Boston, Massachusetts. The unlikely participants in this ritual were a group of ironworkers and cancer-stricken children going in for their chemotherapy treatments. Each day the children who went to the current cancer center would write their names on pieces of paper and then tape the papers up on the windows of a walkway in full view of the construction site. The ironworkers saw the children's names and purposefully and carefully spray painted the names on the steel girders before hoisting them into place. The children and their parents watched with joy as their names became a permanent part of this important building.

Such a simple act, but the awareness it brought to the ironworkers each day was a reminder that what they were doing was more than just building a building. They were bringing hope for a brighter future to so many parents and children alike.

We all want to know that our work makes a difference. Like the ironworkers in this story, a connection to something bigger than our tasks gives us a sense of purpose beyond the day-to-day mechanics of the job. When that connection or sense of purpose is weak or nonexistent, it's easy to feel like a cog in a machine. If you've ever learned of an important company announcement about the company you work for by reading it in the newspaper, you know the feeling of being a cog. We all like to be in the loop. Every day we read in the paper about another round of layoffs coming for one company or another. We can only imagine the thousands of employees who learned of their fate in such an impersonal way.

Communicating to your employees about a service initiative plays a vital role in ensuring its success. If done poorly, the initiative is doomed from the start. Too many organizations, for instance, think that communication simply means an article in the company newsletter: "Well, we announced it in the newsletter, so everyone should know." Leaders are often under the mistaken belief that all employees scour the newsletter for information regarding any new corporate initiative. Effective communication is much more than a newsletter article. *Everything you do* is a potential communication tool—and the more personalized, the better.

The Leadership Action of Communication appears about midway in this book. The fact is, however, that communication is an ongoing part of the service improvement process. It never ends. The previous chapter discussed the development of the Service Philosophy and Service Standards. These now must be communicated to the organization. Communication about the service improvement process, however, should occur earlier, so that employees know what's coming. You can eliminate a lot of frustration with advance communication followed by consistent, ongoing follow-up.

This chapter outlines a communication and awareness plan that helps to ensure that the right message is communicated to the right audience at the right time. Key questions must be answered: How will employees be introduced to the initiative? How will the organization keep everyone informed of what is happening? How will successes be communicated?

Communication Tools

The more communication tools you use, the more likely that people will get the message. First Financial Bankshares, a holding company made up of ten banks, has truly mastered the art of service communication. Messages to employees about the service initiative are everywhere you turn. In addition to bulletin boards, computer screensavers, newsletters, rallies, and recognition events, they have what they call a WOW news release, a short e-mail blast to all employees that shares a story of service excellence in action. Figure 5.1 provides an example of a WOW news release. They've also instituted regular "20-Minute Meeting"

Figure 5.1   WOW News Release Example

topics, which reinforce some aspect of service excellence. Managers receive a facilitator guide for discussing the topic with employees along with interactive participant materials designed to involve employees in the discussion (Figure 5.2).

The point is to be creative in using *every means available* to communicate the Service Philosophy and Service Standards. As you go through the information in this chapter, consider all of the media available in your organization for communicating the message of service excellence.

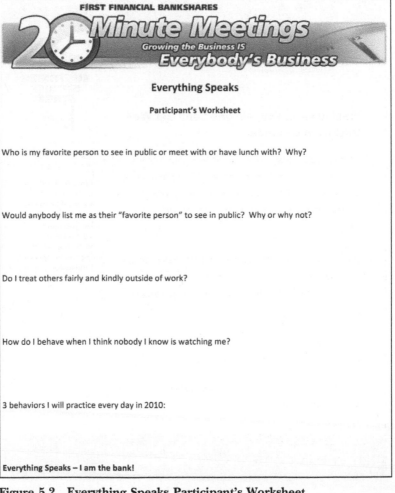

Figure 5.2   Everything Speaks Participant's Worksheet

Stages of Understanding

Nearly everyone experiences three stages of understanding when presented with any new idea, concept, or principle. The three stages are:

1. Awareness—People gain a general understanding that something new is happening.
2. Awkwardness—People try to figure out and apply the new principles/ideas to their own situations. Confusion and frustration are common.
3. Assimilation—The new principles/ideas are incorporated into day-to-day life.

Look at the use of the Internet as an example of the stages of understanding. For those of us old enough that we didn't grow up with the Internet, we started with a very basic understanding of this technology. We had an *awareness* of its existence but didn't really understand what it was all about. All we knew was that it was supposedly something important and useful. Most people had a "we'll see what happens" attitude about the Internet. After a while, we realized that it wasn't going away. More and more people were talking about the Internet and were allegedly getting some benefit from it. So we decided to test the waters a little. Our first few forays onto the Net were probably awkward and uncomfortable. There was likely plenty of frustration and more questions than answers. If we persisted through the *awkward* stage (although some did not), we began to assimilate the Net into our lives. We began using the Internet for such tasks as ordering books, checking the weather, staying on top of the news, communicating with colleagues and friends, checking flight times, and hundreds of other tasks. And with today's social media tools, we can literally share our minute-by-minute activities with anyone who cares to read about them! Back in the *awareness* or *awkwardness* stages no one could have convinced us that we'd be using the Internet as an integral part of our daily lives. But most of us are doing exactly that. In fact, most of us cannot remember how we got along without it.

When launching and sustaining a service initiative, it's important to recognize where people are in the stages of understanding. People have needs that must be fulfilled before they can go on to the next stage. But this principle is violated all the time. We try to rush an initiative without thinking through how employees can best deal with the information. Managers usually rationalize the resulting frustration or apathy by stating, "Our employees just don't get the big picture." It's management's job to communicate the big picture so employees *do* get it. Understanding can stop at the *awareness* or *awkwardness* stages if communication is not executed effectively.

Critical Point

Different levels of the organization go through the stages at different times. The executive team, for example, is usually the group first exposed to a proposed service initiative. They first become aware that something new may be happening. They receive this information from the CEO or whoever is championing the effort. The executives then go through the *awkwardness* stage, trying to deal with the new information and figuring out how to make it workable (or how to make it just go away). Finally, if the executives make it through the first two stages, they begin to assimilate the information and come up with strategies for application. Executives run into serious problems when they forget that other levels of the company are going through, or will go through, the same stages of understanding.

Imagine an executive who, for example, is in the *assimilation* stage. He has worked through the other stages and is now excited and motivated to come up with ideas and solutions. Imagine that he's discussing the service initiative with a mid-level manager who is in the *awkwardness* stage. The mid-level manager is uncomfortable about the whole thing at this point. After all, he's in the *awkwardness* stage. If the executive doesn't understand the different stages and needs, he's likely to be frustrated by the manager's lack of enthusiasm, acceptance, and buy-in. The manager is likely to be frustrated by this executive who seems to be piling one more initiative on the manager's plate. And don't forget about the frontline employee! At this point she doesn't know anything about the initiative but is being asked to join improvement teams, participate in brainstorming sessions, and "be on the bus." She's wondering where this bus came from. She's barely into the *awareness* stage. Everyone ends up frustrated, skeptical of change, and resistant to new initiatives. It's no wonder that so many initiatives fail.

Let's explore each stage of understanding, the mindset that employees have at each stage, and effective communication approaches.

Awareness

There was a time not too long ago when someone had the vision that not all books had to be sold through book stores, or that all news information had to be in print and sold at newsstands. The CEO of Sony pictured a phone fitting into the palm of his hand even though the only car phone in existence at the time was bulky and had to be plugged into the vehicle cigarette lighter outlet. Today, of course, books can be purchased with the click of the mouse. Real-time, up-to-the-minute news is at our fingertips on phones that not only fit in our palms, but also let us take and send pictures, do our banking, play games, and so much more than just talk to our friends. The awareness that these things could be done was just a vision and a vision is only a dream until put into action. At the *awareness* stage, things are an idea, not a reality.

During the awareness stage, the service initiative is just a vision. Employees are simply becoming aware that a service initiative is on the radar screen. There will typically be widespread skepticism. Most employees will think, "Here we go again." At this stage, employees need *information.* They need to understand *why* the organization is focusing on customer service at this particular time and *why* such a focus is important to the organization's future. Effective communication at this point doesn't focus on hows; it focuses on the *whys.*

A full rollout of a detailed plan for the initiative is inappropriate at this point. A full plan hasn't been developed yet. You can only talk about the plan in basic terms at this stage. But it's important to let employees know about the service initiative early in the process. Too many organizations wait until they have a complete plan before they communicate anything. We feel that this approach is a mistake. If you make employees aware of the coming change, and maintain ongoing communication, they won't be surprised when tools, training, and processes are introduced. You'll have already worked through some of the skepticism and doubt.

"Several years ago, our city was planning on instituting mandatory recycling of cans, glass, plastic, and newspapers. For months we were bombarded with information about recycling and why it was important. At first it sounded like one big hassle. But they kept providing us with information. We all eventually got recycling bins and were eased into the process before it became mandatory. For once, they really thought things through. Now I feel guilty when I'm somewhere that doesn't have recycling and I have to throw a soda can in the regular trash."

As the Service Improvement Team commissions the development of the Service Philosophy and Service Standards, we recommend that the team begin crafting and executing the awareness strategy. Remember what people need during the awareness stage—information. They need to know that a customer service initiative is being launched and the reasons for the initiative. Keep in mind that you can't expect enthusiasm or company-wide buy-in at this point. Just start getting the word out.

A hospital, for example, scheduled large group management meetings in which customer service and the upcoming initiative were discussed. This approach gave the managers an opportunity to gain an understanding of the initiative's basic framework, ask questions, and express concerns. The hospital's CEO actively participated in these meetings. Managers were encouraged to talk about the basics of the service initiative with their respective teams. Reading material was suggested to the managers. (At the risk of seeming self-serving, you may want to provide managers with a copy of *this* book to accelerate their understanding of the process.) A couple of weeks later, all frontline employees attended similar meetings that introduced the service initiative. Newsletter articles, hospital-wide e-mails, bulletin boards, and other communication tools supported these meetings. Many organizations have created logos that represent their service improvement efforts, putting them on all initiative-related communications.

Figure 5.3 highlights the components of effective communication during the awareness stage.

You should feel comfortable saying "I don't know" at this stage of the game. You don't have all the answers. Employees are going to help come up with the answers. During the awareness stage, you just want everyone to know that change is coming—stay tuned.

What employees need: *Information*

Communication Approach:
- Why the organization is focusing on customer service.
- The basic approach the organization plans to take with the service initiative.
- Why employee involvement is important to the success of the initiative.
- What type of communication employees can expect to see.
- Commitment from top leadership.

Figure 5.3   Communication During the Awareness Stage

Awkwardness

The second stage, awkwardness, occurs about the time service training (discussed in the next chapter) starts to roll out. During this stage, employees begin to make use of the service improvement tools such as the Everything Speaks Checklist, Service Mapping, Measurement Charts, and so on. Managers conduct brainstorming sessions regarding departmental service improvement. During this time, the Service Improvement Team is ensuring that the training is executed effectively. They are also developing recognition, measurement, and accountability processes. Expect to see and hear plenty of confusion at this stage. Employees will argue about the applicability of the tools and the service effort in general. There may be some finger pointing that goes on.

Since this stage can be the most difficult to work through in keeping everyone focused on the vision, it takes continued visible reinforcement from the top. CEO Linda Watson of LYNX, a bus transit system, wanted to ensure communication of her commitment to the service initiative. A video was created of her stating all the reasons why the company was moving in this direction. While she couldn't be physically present at all the training sessions, this video was shown so that the entire employee population of bus operators and administrative staff would see and hear her personal commitment. She reinforced this during the awkwardness stage by having ASK LINDA boxes placed at all locations so any employee could ask her a question about the service initiative and she would personally respond. The most frequent questions were put in the company newsletter along with her response. Also during this awkwardness stage, acrylic-sleeved frames were placed in all elevators and other high-traffic employee areas. Each month a new graphic communicating the Service Philosophy or an aspect of the Service Standards was created and inserted into the frame.

Please remember that the awkwardness stage is the final stage for many service improvement efforts. Due to the visible confusion and frustration, leadership often thinks the initiative isn't working and brings it to a halt. It's important to recognize the role that awkwardness plays in the process. Employees *need* to wrestle with the concepts. They need to adapt the tools to their world. They need to express their doubts, questions, and confusion. During the awkwardness stage you can expect to see some employees embrace the service improvement effort wholeheartedly. You can expect to see others reject it completely. Most employees approach the effort with some skepticism but are willing to give it a try. The primary mindset at this stage is usually, "How long will it last?"

During the awkwardness stage, employees need *reassurance*. Remember learning to ride your first two-wheeled bike? It's likely that your mom or dad ran along beside you, holding you up as you wobbled down the sidewalk. As you became more confident, they let go. But chances are they still ran along beside you, huffing and puffing, shouting encouragement, reassuring you, and being there in case you fell. Finally, they let you ride off once you felt confident.

Your employees need reassurance that they'll be supported to succeed in the service improvement effort. They need to know that you aren't saying, "Just get on the bike and ride, or else!" Figure 5.4 highlights the components of effective communication during the awkwardness stage.

Employees need to know that the organization is committed to the effort in the long term. If they see communication beginning to drop off, or worse yet stop, credibility is lost very quickly. Keep the service improvement message highly visible as employees work their way through the awkwardness stage.

What employees need: *Reassurance*

Communication Approach:

- Stories and examples of service excellence in action.
- Coaching on using the service improvement tools.
- Recognition of employees who are providing great service.
- Ongoing commitment to getting input from employees about the service improvement initiative.

Figure 5.4 Communication During the Awkwardness Stage

Assimilation

The *assimilation* stage is characterized by a feeling that there is a consistent understanding of the service initiative and that service excellence behaviors are becoming "inculturated." During this stage the service improvement tools have become part of the normal operation, everyone has attended the appropriate training, and accountability processes have been implemented. There may be some left-over skepticism from the earlier stages, but, overall, most everyone is on board.

You can expect to reach this point 12 to 18 months into the effort (as long as you stick it out through the awkwardness stage and have truly implemented the processes described in this book). The mindset of employees at this stage is likely to be, "so what else is new?" There's a real danger of losing momentum or allowing service improvement communication to go stale. Many may not even be aware of the impact of the service improvement effort; they've simply assimilated it into their behaviors. Many may not realize how unusual it is for an organization to take on a significant cultural change and see it through.

Several years ago we worked with a resort organization on a large service improvement effort. They were very committed and followed through on most, if not all, of the improvement processes. During a later conversation with a member of the management team, he expressed disappointment with the initiative. He felt not much had changed. "How are your business results lately?" we asked. He said they were better than ever. "How about customer satisfaction?" Again, better than ever. Employee turnover was down, morale was strong, and they were expanding into new markets. Why was this manager disappointed? Because the initiative had been assimilated into the daily operation. It didn't *feel* like anything new was happening because service excellence was now "business as usual."

Upon reaching the assimilation stage, it's important to keep service communication fresh, creative, and ongoing. Don't let up! During the assimilation stage employees need communication regarding *what's new*. About the time you reach the assimilation stage is when the Service Improvement Team typically transitions to new members. Communicate the changing of the guard. Let everyone know what has been accomplished since the beginning of the initiative. The new members of the Service Improvement Team should take a fresh look at the communications process. Remember those posters that were put up during the launch? Are they looking worn and faded? Is the company newsletter still referring to the "new service initiative"? Employees need to see that service is and will remain a top priority. Fresh, creative communication can assist with this. In a very public way the CEO should recognize what has been accomplished but also recommit him or herself to keeping service excellence a top priority.

Kim Poulton, executive sponsor of the Service Improvement Team for Florida's Turnpike Enterprise, was emphatic that every employee would represent the organization's Service Standards consistently every day. Not an easy task, considering there are 4,600 employees, employed by more than 12 different corporate entities, deployed on a 608-mile road network.

Each quarter, Florida's Turnpike Enterprise's 320 managers receive a booklet of communication strategies, all focused on one Service Standard for the quarter. The booklet for the quarter contains three communications strategies (one per month) that the manager is expected to deliver. It's up to the manager how to deliver messages, based on the needs of the specific team. The booklet includes an overview of the plan, a reminder of the Service Standards, a one-page article for each topic, and suggestions for delivering the message to a group. The managers also receive a "toolbox" containing supplemental materials such as display posters, quotations, and Internet references. A feedback card is included for managers to return to the Service Improvement Team each month with a description of how they had delivered their message and how many employees they had reached.

Walt Disney World has always focused on continuous improvement of their guest services. At one time they began an initiative they called "Performance Excellence." An important part of the effort was a yearly best practices fair. Departments from all over the company were invited to create booths highlighting things that they were doing to create service excellence. Internal and external service were both highlighted. Cast members explored the fair to see what was happening around the company. Everyone, especially the executive team, was blown away by the things that were happening. The results were fantastic:

- Best practices were shared around the entire organization.
- Guests were continually wowed by improved service approaches.
- Cast members saw that service was an ongoing priority.
- Management was exposed to the creativity of the cast for elevating the guest experience.

These best practice fairs were used as a tool to creatively communicate "what's new."

Figure 5.5 highlights the components of effective communication during the assimilation stage.

Your main objective during the assimilation stage should be to keep the momentum of the customer service effort going. Be creative and relentless. Keep in mind that radically new service ideas will travel through the awareness and awkwardness stages again before being assimilated into day-to-day behaviors. It's a never-ending process.

What employees need: *What's new about the service effort*
Communication Approach:
- Direction and priorities of the Service Improvement Team.
- Success stories—service heroes.
- Best practices.
- Satisfaction measurement results.
- Refreshed and renewed collateral materials.
- Ongoing involvement opportunities.

Figure 5.5   Communication During the Assimilation Stage

Concluding Thoughts

Ongoing communication of the service improvement effort is critical to its overall success. Communication, however, must be orchestrated so that the right message goes to the right audience at the right time. It's important to recognize that each stage of understanding (awareness, awkwardness, and assimilation) has unique needs and must be handled appropriately. Many service improvement initiatives fail due to the fact that organizations don't recognize the stages of understanding or realize that different parts of the organization may be in different stages. By planning a communication strategy appropriately, with employee needs in mind, you can keep momentum up and ensure that service improvement becomes a way of life in the organization.

Service Improvement Team Action Steps

- Assign this Leadership Action to a Service Improvement Team member who is familiar with your organization's formal communications processes.
- Develop a plan of awareness activities for the next 6 to 9 months.
- Order the necessary materials to carry out the awareness plan.
- Prepare agenda items for management meetings to ensure there is ongoing discussion regarding the process.
- Communicate and encourage use of all service improvement tools.
- Collect "wow" ideas and report feedback to other areas.
- Collaborate with other Leadership Action chairpersons in communicating their progress and successes.
- Recognize that new ideas, processes, and concepts will travel through the stages of understanding—awareness, awkwardness, and assimilation.

- Be creative in your use of all forms of communications media.
- Recognize that skepticism and apathy are normal responses to initial communications.

Pitfalls to Avoid

- Don't rely on the company newsletter as the only communication medium.
- Don't assume or expect that everyone goes through the stages of understanding at the same time.
- Don't wait until the service improvement initiative is fully planned before beginning the communication process. Prepare people for what is coming.
- Don't just communicate the facts. Tell stories!
- Don't let communication go stale as time goes on.

Chapter Six

TRAINING AND EDUCATION

Think about this unique approach to customer service training used by a general manager of an upscale restaurant. He wanted to make sure that new employees understand at a gut level the importance of their jobs:

"In the restaurant business, employees hired as dishwashers are usually considered the lowest rung on the ladder—a job with a revolving door. Most managers devote little, if any, time to training their dishwashers. Not in this manager's case. After hiring a dishwasher, he arranges for them to have a nice breakfast or lunch at the restaurant to discuss job responsibilities, expectations, and questions the new-hire might have. A nice meal is arranged—one that would exceed the expectations of the employee. The food presented is excellent and attractive. The manager has done a little pre-work, however. The dishes that set the table have dried food on them. Lipstick coats the rims of the water glasses. Forks, knives, and spoons are spotted and dirty. The manager watches for the reaction of the new dishwasher and, when he sees the look of surprise (or disgust), he makes his point. 'It doesn't matter how great our food is; if *you* don't pay attention to detail, the customer experience is lousy. Your job is critical to our restaurant's success.'"

It would be hard to come up with a better way to make the manager's point. That newly hired dishwasher knows at a gut level how important his job is. He has seen through the lens of the customer. *That's* great training!

Chapter 5 focused on communicating the service initiative. We discussed getting the word out about the initiative, introducing the Service Philosophy and Service Standards, and keeping the initiative constantly on the radar screen. This chapter will outline a training strategy for ensuring a consistent understanding of the initiative and everyone's role in its execution.

The Role of Training

We have to make a disclaimer early in this chapter. Training is not the answer to every customer service issue. It may be part of the answer, but only a part. Training cannot teach an employee how to be friendly. By the time someone is old enough to have a job, he or she is either friendly or not. Training can only teach a friendly employee how to be friendly in a way that's consistent with your culture. If he or she's not friendly to begin with, training is worthless. So, *hiring* the right person (discussed in the next chapter) is the key to successful training. As some companies are now saying, "We hire for attitude; we train for skill."

Let's look at a grocery store cashier who is unfriendly with customers. She's abrupt and irritable. Let's say that the store manager tells the employee, "If you're not friendly to the next customer, you're fired." Lo and behold, the employee *is* friendly to the next customer. This indicates a motivation problem, not a training problem. Yet, many managers will send this cashier off to smile training and will get little or no return on the investment. What the cashier might really need is a dose of accountability (discussed in Chapter 11).

We don't mean to say that training isn't important—it is important. Training provides a forum for your employees to actually wrestle with specific service principles and begin to apply those principles to their own jobs. Training helps your organization to consistently express what service in your company is supposed to look like, sound like, and feel like. Most importantly, service training allows your employees to talk about their own experiences and connect to the service initiative at a personal and *emotional* level, not just an intellectual one. Without an emotional connection by the employee, the principles have just been taught; they haven't been learned. Real learning in a customer service program brings out what's already in the employee and helps them to use it effectively.

When a service improvement process is first rolled out, the training sessions can be somewhat of a pep rally to get employees excited about the effort. Don't discount the pep rally idea because it appears too touchy-feely. If employees don't feel an emotional connection to the effort, it is hard to change behaviors. Also (and we stress this), there *must* be mechanisms beyond the training that demonstrate the organization's commitment to supporting the desired service behaviors. Management must live their commitment; employees will follow. So, again, we say that service training is *part* of the solution.

Commitment to Training

Observing the role that training and education plays in organizations highlights an interesting dynamic. On the one hand, most leaders will say that proper training is one of the keys to organizational success. On the other hand, when things get tight, training dollars are usually the first to get cut from the budget. It's easy to cut training dollars. One simply removes the dollars from the budget. World-class companies, on the other hand, are committed to making the investment in training. A colleague of ours effectively expressed the importance of commitment:

"I was teaching a seminar for a group of executives and I was talking about the importance of training. I talked about the need to get everyone in the company on the same page. One of the executives raised his hand and stood up with a question. 'I run a business that has pretty high employee turnover; it's just part of the industry. What if I spend all this time and effort to train an employee and he leaves?' I guess my response was kind of smart-mouthed, but I responded back, 'What if you *don't* spend the time and effort to train the employee and he stays?' I guess I made my point because he laughed and said, 'I hadn't thought of it that way.'"

It seems painless to reduce the training budget on a spreadsheet. You just change the number. Down the road, however, the pain does come. The pain comes in the form of increased customer complaints, increased process errors, increased employee turnover, decreased employee morale, and decreased customer loyalty. All because of how easy it is to change a number on a spreadsheet. Commitment to the service improvement effort means a commitment to the training effort. World-class service organizations don't look at training as an expense; they look at it as an investment.

Training doesn't mean simply sending employees to classes. As you'll see later in this chapter, training can and must take many forms. Training sessions, however, are important to the service improvement process. In the remainder of this chapter we'll explore the training needed for various levels of employees in the organization, the service component of new-hire orientation, and ongoing training.

Employee Levels and Training

In just about every customer service seminar we conduct, someone ambushes us on a break and exclaims, "My boss should hear this!" Someone right behind them will say, "My employees need to hear this!'' Hopefully, they feel that they need to hear it themselves, too. The point is, everyone needs to hear the service message—but in a way that's meaningful to them in their roles. Each level in the organization has specific needs and questions that are unique to their situation.

Our recommendation is to hold separate training sessions for different levels of the organization. All service improvement training will have the same core components regardless of employee level. Subjects such as the Service Philosophy and Service Standards, for example, must be consistent across the board. The difference is in the responsibility each level has regarding the service improvement process.

The job levels described here and the approach will vary depending on the size of the organization. You may decide that, because of your structure, it's appropriate to have everyone together for the training, regardless of level. You clearly know your situation much better than we do and we again encourage you to adapt this material to your organization.

Executive-Level Training

Executive-level participants need to know how the service initiative meshes with the long-term plans of the company. They need to know about the tools that are available to them for implementing the service initiative. The training should help them understand how to handle the initial skepticism that will no doubt rear its head among the troops. They also need to know that there is room for their input. If an executive feels cornered into an initiative and has no chance to give an opinion, you can bet that he or she is going to make the training miserable for everyone—especially the trainer.

Figure 6.1 provides an agenda for an executive-level training session. You'll see that it's a 2-day session. We can hear the howls of protest: "I can't get my executive team together for 2 hours much less 2 days!" We've had clients insist that their executives can grasp

DAY 1

8:00 AM–8:30 AM	**Arrival/Breakfast**
8:30 AM–8:45 AM	**CEO Kickoff**

- The role of the service improvement effort in the overall company strategy

8:45 AM–10:15 AM   **Components of a Service-Driven Culture/Language of Service**

- The customer service model:
  - Lens of the customer
  - Everything Speaks
  - Create a Wow
  - Processes

10:15 AM–10:30 AM   **Break**

10:30 AM–10:45 AM   **Introduction of the Nine Leadership Actions**

10:45 AM–12 noon   **Leadership Action 1—The Service Improvement Team**

- Introduce members of the Service Improvement Team
- Purpose of the Service Improvement Team
- Executive expectations of the Service Improvement Team
- Service Improvement Team expectations of executives

12 noon–1:00 PM   **Lunch**

1:00 PM–2:30 PM   **Leadership Action 2—Service Improvement Core Tools**

- Overview of the Service Philosophy and Service Standards
- How the Service Philosophy and Service Standards were developed
- Service Mapping
- Everything Speaks Checklist

Figure 6.1   Executive-Level Service Improvement Training Agenda (Go to www.UnleashingExcellence.com to download a customizable copy of this form.)

- Examples/Questions
- Application

2:30 PM–2:45 PM   **Break**

2:45 PM–3:30 PM   **Leadership Action 3—Communication**

- Overview of service improvement communication strategy
- Stages of Understanding
- Executive role in initial and ongoing awareness

3:30 PM–4:15 PM   **Leadership Action 4—Training and Education**

- Introduction of the overall service improvement training plan
- Registration process
- Pre-training expectations (what trainees should know before attending)
- High-level overview of manager and frontline training sessions
- Review changes to new-hire orientation
- Executive role in training support

4:15 PM–4:30 PM   **Wrap Day 1**

DAY 2

8:00 AM–8:30 AM   **Breakfast**

8:30 AM–9:00 AM   **Review of Day 1/Q&A**

9:00 AM–10:00 AM   **Leadership Action 5—Interviewing and Selection**

- Selecting for talent
- Modeling service excellence in the interview process
- Executive role in Interview and Selection process
  - Staffing with A-players

10:00 AM–10:15 AM   **Break**

10:15 AM–11:00 AM   **Leadership Action 6—Measurement**

- Overview of baseline Measurement plan
- Potential day-to-day service Measurements
- Executive role in Measurement process

Figure 6.1   (*Continued*)

11:00 AM–12 noon	**Leadership Action 7—Recognition**
	• The role of Recognition in service improvement
	• Current Recognition tools in place/needed adjustments
	• Executive role in Recognition
12 noon–1:00 PM	**Lunch**
1:00 PM–1:45 PM	**Leadership Action 8—Service Obstacle System**
	• Discussion of potential barriers to service improvement
	• Overview of the service improvement process
	• Executive role in service improvement
1:45 PM–2:30 PM	**Leadership Action 9—Management Accountability**
	• Importance of "walking the talk"
	• Overview of Management Accountability processes
	• Executive role in Management Accountability
2:30 PM–3:00 PM	**Break**
3:00 PM–4:30 PM	**Executive To Do's**
	• Expectations for executive team
	- Ensure that all managers and frontline employees attend the service improvement training
	- Prepare your managers for attendance in the upcoming manager workshops
	- Begin using the service improvement tools—i.e., the Service Map—Everything Speaks Checklist, in your own areas
	- Begin all meetings with service-related issues
	- Begin recognizing excellent service behaviors as soon as you see them
	- Identify potential areas for service improvement within your area of responsibility
	- Walk the customer service talk. Be a role model
	- Catch people doing things right
4:30 PM	**CEO Wrap-up**

Figure 6.1 (*Continued*)

the service improvement concepts in a 90-minute overview. True, the participants probably can grasp the concepts in that amount of time. It's critical, however, that executives have more than a *grasp*. What's needed is true *commitment*. If executives can't commit significant time at the beginning of this important process, the likelihood of their ongoing commitment is slim. Besides, to be effective, executives need to hash out the issues and come to grips with what success requires. That can't be done in 90 minutes.

The agenda in Figure 6.1 concludes with a to-do list for the executives to take away from the training. The participants should be very clear about what behaviors are being asked of them. We learned this the hard way with one client organization.

During a 2-day executive training session, we painstakingly took the participants step-by-step through the service initiative and Leadership Actions. We thought we did an excellent job. We were wrong. The executives were never told what we were asking them to *do*. Some participants walked away from the session confused about what was being asked of them. There was even a hint that the entire service improvement effort may be postponed due to the lack of support from some of the executive team.

Fortunately, the president of the company took a stand in favor of moving forward, but it took about 2 weeks to clear up the confusion and proceed with the process. Learn from our mistake and be crystal clear regarding the specific behaviors and actions you're asking of the executive team. Those to-do's listed in Figure 6.1 were painfully earned—they're important.

Manager-Level Training

The main difference between executive training and manager training is that the manager training is more tactical. Managers are the ones responsible for transforming the service concepts into day-to-day actions. That's not an easy job for managers who are already busy.

If you've been a middle manager, you know how tough the job can be. You're bombarded from all sides with initiatives, problems, programs, budgets, and a thousand other "priorities." Many managers are going to see this service initiative as one more thing that they're going to have to cram into an already crammed schedule. The training is going to need to help managers deal with that issue. If the executives are doing their service improvement jobs as discussed in the previous section, managers *should* have some knowledge of the effort when they attend the manager training sessions.

Some managers, of course, will arrive to the training with no idea of what's going on, no interest in attending the training, and ticked off that their work is piling up at the office while they attend. Many of the managers will have the attitude, "Here we go again—another program-of-the-month." You can't blame them for feeling skeptical. Most managers have seen dozens of programs come and go.

Accept that this attitude will be there to some degree. We even recommend agreeing with these skeptical managers. Acknowledge that there have been programs-of-the-month in the past. Express that the difference with this effort lies in the processes that are to be implemented that make service improvement part of the company culture. Mechanisms will be put in place to assist with the effort. Keep in mind that we're not naïve. Making these claims won't result in the skeptics suddenly beaming with enthusiasm and proclaiming, "Well, okay then! Bring it on!" By addressing the issue head on, however, you'll have won a few points for not being overly Pollyanna about the whole thing.

The reality, of course, is that most managers' plates are already full. And here comes this trainer cheerfully asking them to do more! The standard line that trainers use is, "This will actually save you time. You'll be able to focus on the things that really matter." The response of most managers is, "Will someone please tell me the things that *don't* matter? No one has ever told me, 'Oh, you don't need to do *that* part of the job anymore.' I just keep getting more work piled on me." Don't fall into the "this will save you time" trap. It's better to acknowledge that the service improvement process *will* require additional effort in the beginning. The quicker managers get their employees involved and implement the service improvement tools, the quicker the effort is carried by everyone, thus lightening the load. But being world-class is *not* easy.

Figure 6.2 outlines an agenda for a 1-day managers' training program. It deals with a lot of the issues and concerns we've addressed and gives the managers a chance to vent, question, wrestle with, and (hopefully) accept their responsibilities in the service initiative. Like with the executive-level sessions, make sure that the managers are clear about what is being asked of them.

Frontline-Level Training

Let's admit one thing right at the beginning of this section—most frontline employees *love* to go to training seminars. Why? Because any time spent in a training class is time away from the job. During that seminar they don't have to answer phones, handle customer complaints, stock shelves, or whatever. They feel that their main objective in the seminar is to stay awake. The only frontline employees that we've run into who hate going to training seminars are secretaries and sales people working on commission. Secretaries hate it because their work piles up while they're gone. Commission sales people hate it because to them time is literally money. If training is going to truly have an impact on the frontline, it's got to be great.

Figure 6.3 provides an agenda for a training session for frontline employees. You might have noticed that the timeframe for the sessions keeps getting shorter (2 days for executives; 1 day for managers; 2 hours for frontline employees). We've had many people tell us, "This seems backwards. Shouldn't the people on the frontline get the most customer service training?" We love this question because it leads to a key point. Classroom training is

9:00 AM–9:30 AM	**Welcome Session/Introduction**
	• Objectives of the service improvement process
	• Overview of service improvement process to date
	• Benefits to the individual and the organization
9:30 AM–10:30 AM	**Components of a Service-Driven Culture/ Language of Service**
	• The customer service model
	- Lens of the customer
	- Everything Speaks
	- Create a Wow
	- Review Service Philosophy and Service Standards
	- Processes:
	- Examples
	- Service Mapping
	- Everything Speaks Checklist
10:30 AM–10:45 AM	**Break**
10:45 AM–12 noon	**Manager Tool 1—Service Mapping**
	• Overview of service mapping technique
	• Examples of service mapping
	• Group application—case study
12 noon–1:00 PM	**Lunch**
1:00 PM–1:30 PM	**Manager Tool 2—Service Measurement**
	• Overview of baseline measurement plan
	• Examples of day-to-day service measurements
	• Group application—case study
1:30 PM–2:15 PM	**Manager Tool 3—Everything Speaks Checklist**
	• Review checklist (or draft of checklist)
	• Guidelines for effective use of the checklist
	• Group practice
2:15 PM–2:30 PM	**Break**
2:30 PM–3:00 PM	**Manager Tool 4—Service Obstacle System**
	• Discussion of potential barriers to service improvement

Figure 6.2 Manager-Level Service Improvement Training Agenda (Go to www.UnleashingExcellence.com to download a customizable copy of this form.)

- Review of manager's role in continuous service improvement
- Overview of tools and resources for improvement

3:00 PM–4:30 PM   **Manager Tool 5—Manager's Action Plan**
(Break as needed)   - Discuss need for manager to "walk the talk"
- Review manager tools
- Completion of individual action plans:
  - Tool implementation plan
  - Date commitments to begin

4:30 PM–4:45 PM   **Wrap-up**

Figure 6.2   (*Continued*)

only the tip of the iceberg. If executives and managers are doing the job discussed in *their* training sessions, they are *constantly* training their employees through what they do, say, recognize, and a hundred other ways.

Training for frontline employees should:

1. Ensure consistent understanding of the service improvement process.
2. Share best practices regarding service excellence.
3. Develop personal action plans for service excellence.
4. Communicate next steps.

One word describes the ideal delivery of the frontline sessions: interactive. More than any other type of training, service training sessions must demonstrate respect for the expertise of the participants. Frontline employees deal with the real world every day, and having a "corporate type" *telling* them about customer service is insulting. The participants must be involved in the session, providing input, opinions, and challenges. The discussion is the key. And please, whatever you do, do *not* create a video of service vignettes that demonstrate the proper method for an employee-customer interaction. The typical service video contains such ridiculous dialogue as:

15 min.	**Welcome/Opening**

- Service-oriented participation activity
- Objectives of the service improvement process
- Overview of the service improvement process to date
- Significance of the process to the company and employees

10 min.	**Introduction of the Customer Service Model**
20 min.	**The "Lens of the Customer"**

- Definition of the "lens of the customer"
- Interactive case study identifying behaviors that demonstrate an understanding of the customer's lens
- Service mapping

20 min.	**"Everything Speaks"**

- Definition of "everything speaks"
- Interactive identification of environmental distracters
- The Everything Speaks Checklist

20 min.	**"Creating Service Wows"**

- Service wows in the real world
- Interactive identification of behaviors that frustrate customers
- Participant discussion of local best practices for exceeding expectations

20 min.	**Introduction of Service Philosophy and Service Standards**

- Quick overview of the Service Philosophy and Service Standards
- Interactive exercise applying the standards to specific situations
- Individual action plans
  - Personal application of the Service Standards

15 min.	**Interactive Review of Content/Next Steps**

2 hours total

Figure 6.3   Frontline-Level Service Improvement Training Agenda (Go to www.UnleashingExcellence.com to download a customizable copy of this form.)

"Oh yes, Mrs. Jones. I see the problem right here. I'm so sorry this occurred and I will take care of it right away. Is there anything else I can do for you today? No? Well, we certainly thank you for your business."

The silent and not-so-silent guffaws of the participants provide clues as to the realism of these vignettes. The underlying feeling is, "Life just ain't that way!" Rarely are service situations so black and white. Varying shades of gray best describes the clarity of service situations experienced by frontline employees. When a training session contains an unrealistic perspective of the world, credibility quickly vanishes. It is much better to respect the experience of the participants by tapping into their expertise.

Customer Facing and Back Office/Support Staff Issues

We've all attended training classes made up of participants representing such extremely diverse functions that there was little common ground for useful discussion. There are some good reasons for having customer facing and support staff in the same training sessions. But usually a lot of valuable time is spent trying to include examples and discussion points that apply to everyone's job function. The session ends up either bogged down or too generic. No matter how hard you try to be inclusive, some participants will feel that the discussion "just doesn't apply to me."

For the service improvement training addressed in this book, we recommend that you segment the training sessions by customer facing employees and support staff employees, especially at the frontline level. Yes, we know that segmenting the groups could result in an "us versus them" perception (which may already exist). We know there's great value in employees understanding the roles of other employees. In many training efforts we would heartily recommend a mix of customer facing and support staff employees, but not for this effort. You'll have to decide what makes sense for your organization based on size, structure, and culture.

Conducting the Training Sessions

You've probably heard the statistics before, but they're worth repeating. According to a study conducted by the U.S. Department of Health, Education, and Welfare, learners remember:

- 10 percent of what they read.
- 20 percent of what they hear.
- 30 percent of what they see.
- 50 percent of what they see and hear.
- 70 percent of what they say.
- 90 percent of what they say and do.

There are other, varying statistics out there, but the point is clear. Make training *active*. Sitting employees down for 2 hours (or 2 days) and lecturing them isn't going to accomplish anything. Getting employees to talk, argue, experiment, play, and solve real-life problems has a much greater chance of influencing behaviors.

During an engagement with a resort organization, we were conducting a series of 2-hour frontline service training sessions. At the conclusion of one of the sessions, a housekeeper came up and said, "I was ready to hate this when they told me to come to the class. I just looked at it as a 2-hour break. But it was realistic and it was fun. I learned a lot. Thanks." This was positive reinforcement coming from someone in a tough job—housekeeping. Our hope, of course, was that this housekeeper's manager reinforced the content on a daily basis.

You want the training to create a buzz around the organization. When employees go back to their workplaces and their coworkers ask them about the training, you want them to respond, "It was great, you've got to go." The only way they're going to respond that way is if the training is realistic, active, and fun. On the other hand, we've all asked colleagues how a seminar was and they said, "Best 2 hours sleep I've had in weeks." That's not the kind of press you need.

When asked, most executives will quickly state, "Don't do any of those training activities or games during the executive session.

Our executives don't go for that stuff. Just give us the info." Then, when we do conduct an activity, it's great to watch these same serious executives get totally into the activity and ask for the instructions so they can conduct it for their own teams. People are people and we all like to have fun. The times that we've seen well-run activities fail is when there was no clear learning from the activity (which means it wasn't well run after all).

The Leader's Role in Customer Service Training

We were conducting a customer service program for a group of executives. The CEO of the company did a fantastic job kicking off the program. He stressed the importance of the message, the commitment of the company, and the vital role that customer service will play in the company's future. It was more than we could've dreamed—until he sat down.

Throughout the program he constantly disappeared to take phone calls. He accepted cell phone calls right in the middle of the session and began talking as he left the room. During the session he reviewed paperwork and worked on the details of his schedule. Make no mistake about it—every single participant in that room was watching how seriously the CEO took the training.

During each level of training, an executive or member of the management team will usually introduce the session, stressing the organization's commitment to customer service. Following the kickoff, the best thing the CEO or manager can do is to sit at one of the front tables in the room, listen intently, participate appropriately, offer insights periodically, and take copious notes. Everyone is watching.

Ongoing Training

We're often asked the question, "How often should refresher service training be offered?" The answer, of course, is that refresher training should occur every day. Training isn't just about formal, classroom sessions. As a matter of fact, real training is *never* about formal, classroom sessions.

What happens *after* the training sessions really determines the success or failure of the service improvement effort. Time spent in the classroom is simply a launching pad for the day-to-day application and reinforcement of the service principles. A real-life story helps to illustrate the power of never-ending training:

We're acquainted with the former general manager of an upscale restaurant in Florida who made training a significant component of his restaurant's success formula. He had every new employee attend a general company orientation but recognized that it was *his* responsibility to support and supplement the education his employees received. So he spent 15 minutes *every* day educating all employees (front-of-house and back-of-house). If he wasn't there, the assistant manager conducted the training session. Three topics were covered in these short sessions: wine, food, and service. He trained servers from all walks of life to be world-class food and wine experts. Every employee on every shift knew how to describe all menu items in a way that highlighted the reason that it was special (menu items vary depending on season). His servers knew the perfect wine to accompany the meal a guest had ordered. Servers could describe the freshness of ingredients in a way that would literally make your mouth water. Customer service issues were discussed that included recognizing performance, providing showmanship tips (how to describe the wine list is truly an art), or anything else he felt deserved attention. The impact of these daily educational moments were impressive:

- Wine revenue represented 30+ percent of total sales at his restaurant. Beverage sales in similar restaurants average only 10 to 15 percent of sales.
- 65 percent of the original staff were still with the restaurant (7 years later). This is in an industry that averages nearly 200 percent turnover per year.
- The restaurant was (and still is) consistently rated as one of the best in Central Florida.

Education, in all its forms, pays off when it's focused, sincere, and *ongoing*. Most world-class organizations quickly indicate training and education as keys to their success. However, it isn't simply a matter of sending employees to classes and checking training off your to-do list. It's about using educational opportunities to strategically deepen the culture of the organization.

Should refresher classes be offered yearly? Yes, since yearly refresher sessions provide an opportunity to review progress made and to discuss ideas for further progress. Yearly refresher classes also provide employees with the chance to hear about what other areas of the company are doing in regard to service improvement. Figure 6.4 suggests an agenda for a 2-hour annual refresher class, but make no mistake about it—what happens in the employees' work areas every day is one hundred times more powerful than anything that takes place in a class.

New-Hire Orientation

Imagine you've just hired a bright new employee. This employee is excited about getting the job but also a little nervous. The employee goes to new-hire orientation and listens for hours to information about:

- what he can get fired for.
- what does and does not constitute sexual harassment.
- the maze of benefits available for an ungodly variety of copayments (isn't it exciting to hear about "accidental death and dismemberment" on your first day?).
- how to clock in and out.

Then, the instructor leaves the room after popping in a 10-minute video about customer service (containing those wonderful service vignettes). This agenda constitutes 99 percent of the new-hire orientation programs in existence. This type of program sucks all life out of the new hire and makes him wonder what company the recruiter was talking about during the interview.

10 min.   **Welcome Session/Overview**
- "In this workshop we will:"
  - Discuss progress made with the service initiative
  - Review core elements of the initiative
  - Discuss taking customer service to the next level
- Table activity—Best example of creating a great customer experience since launch of the initiative

10 min.   **Progress to Date**
- Overall purpose of the initiative
- What the Service Improvement Team has accomplished
  - Business results

20 min.   **Review of the Service Excellence Model**

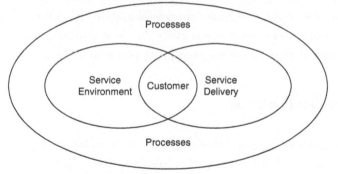

- Customer—look at everything "through the lens of the customer"
  - Examples of "through the lens of the customer" behaviors
    - Pop-up examples from participants
- Environment—pay attention to detail because "everything speaks"
  - Examples of how "everything speaks" applies to your work environment
    - Pop-up examples from participants
- Delivery—create a wow
  - Examples of creating customer service wows
    - Refer to examples from opening activity
    - Additional pop-up examples from participants

Figure 6.4 Service Excellence Refresher Workshop (Go to www. UnleashingExcellence.com to download a customizable copy of this form.)

20 min.   **Service Philosophy and Standards**

- Contest for correctly reciting the Service Philosophy and Standards word-for-word
- Table activity applying each of the standards to the specific roles of participants
  - Group report outs

5 min.   **Brief Recap of the Leadership Actions**

1. Service Improvement Team
2. Service Improvement Core Tools
3. Communication
4. Training and Education
5. Interviewing and Selection
6. Measurement
7. Recognition
8. Service Obstacle System
10. Accountability

45 min.   **Participant Rating on Success of Leadership Actions 3–10**

- Flipchart pages taped to wall with Leadership Actions (Flipchart Example)

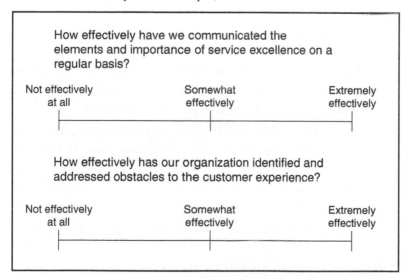

- Provide each participant with enough "sticky dots" for each of the Leadership Actions

Figure 6.4 (*Continued*)

- Have each participant place a sticky dot on the charts where they feel current organizational performance lies
- Facilitate discussion around trends/patterns that appear from the input
- Based on the discussion and input, what top three actions should the Service Improvement Team take to elevate service to the next level?
  - Table discussion
  - Group report out
- Personal Application—What three things are you willing to do to take customer service to the next level in your own performance?
  - Individual report out from 2–3 volunteers

10 min.   **Conclusion/Next Steps**
- Review strategy for moving forward
  - Leadership Actions still to be implemented
  - Evolution of Service Improvement Team
  - Planned activities
  - Workshop wrap-up and call to action

2 hours total

Figure 6.4   (*Continued*)

An employee's first day is the most important day of the employee's tenure with your company. Anything that does or does not happen on the first day remains with the employee forever. Be sure to adapt the frontline service training session for inclusion in your company's new-hire orientation. If you only provide service training for your current employees and make no adjustment to your orientation process, it's like bailing water out of a boat with a hole in it. New employees just keep pouring into the organization without exposure to the service concepts we've been discussing. Certainly, they'll get some of the information from their managers, if their managers have bought in and are on the ball. But starting a new employee out on the right foot with consistent information regarding the company's approach to service is priceless. You don't get that chance back. While you're rolling out the frontline service improvement training, be sure that new-hire orientation is adjusted to prominently feature the same content.

Client company First Financial Bankshares, a holding company made up of ten banks, completely revamped their new-hire orientation program after the launch of their service initiative. According to the organization's Training and Education champion, Doyle Lee, they found that over the years their orientation program had become a training dumping ground for every compliance issue or policy/procedure change that came along (a common problem). They've since moved many of the elements from new-hire orientation to on-the-job training, where the new employee will better understand the context of how those elements apply to their job. Other components formerly in orientation have been included in comprehensive online training programs, again ensuring that the information is presented when the new employee is better able to understand it. And they've strategically saved the final 2½ hours of orientation to devote solely to the details of their customer service initiative, "Customer Service First." The reason for placement of the segment is that they want their new employees to leave orientation with the importance of customer service uppermost in mind. In addition to the items outlined in Figure 6.3, they also discuss such topics as eye contact, body language, and vocal quality. In order to make the content especially relevant, before each orientation class the instructors review the participant list and include customer service examples for *every* job represented in the class.

Another client, Cool Cuts 4 Kids, a hair salon chain that focuses on children as their primary customer, developed a fun and creative orientation for all their new employees. Because their Service Standards focus on being playful and having fun so the children would enjoy getting their hair cut, the orientation sets this tone by making the training playful and fun. The Service Mapping discussion becomes an adventure map moving from one point of contact to another. Measurement is introduced in a format similar to the Candy Land game. The graphics all tie to the culture they're looking to create with their customers. Melissa Mattern, the VP of Salon Operations and Service Improvement Team chairperson, says, "By creating an orientation that is fun, innovative, and uniquely geared toward the kidcentric business, we can actively engage new employees from day one as to what is expected from them in terms of job performance and service behaviors."

On-the-Job Training

Ralph Waldo Emerson famously said: "I pay the school master, but 'tis the school boys that educate my son."

Emerson is saying that people learn from what's happening around them. You may have a great orientation program, but that new hire is going to spend a lot of time with other employees once he or she is on the job. That's where the real learning will take place.

Following orientation, a newly hired employee is usually paired with an experienced (we hope) employee to learn the mechanics of the job. You can imagine how many times this experienced employee says to the charged-up new hire, "Forget all that stuff they taught you in orientation. I'll tell you how things really work." The new employee then watches as the "old hand" is rude to customers and coworkers and complains about the management. All your hard work on the service initiative just imploded.

Selecting trainers is one of the most important decisions you'll make. They have a massive impact on the success of your organization.

"I showed up to work after my day of orientation. My supervisor didn't even know I was going to be there and didn't seem too happy about the surprise. She said, 'I guess I'll just put you with one of our experienced associates; he'll teach you what to do.' I couldn't believe the guy they stuck me with. He was lazy and more interested in telling me about his partying habits than how to do the job. He wouldn't help customers—he went the other way when he saw them. After 3 hours I was ready to quit."

Can you imagine how demoralizing that situation must be? The scary thing is that it happens all the time.

Choose trainers with care. They have to be technically excellent, of course. But are they customer service role models? Do they live your Service Philosophy and Service Standards consistently? Being a trainer should be a position of honor, not a position of convenience. Which of your employees would you most love to clone? Shouldn't they be the ones training your new hires how to do the job?

Concluding Thoughts

"A great teacher never strives to explain his vision—he simply invites you to stand beside him and see for yourself."

—Reverend E. Inman

While we do believe that great teachers explain their vision, we also agree with the essence of Reverend Inman's quote. We've stressed that effective training can only bring out what is already in an employee and help him or her become even more effective in your company's environment.

Really, this whole book is about training. Involving employees in developing the service initiative, communicating constantly, holding seminars, measuring, holding employees accountable— it's all training.

Effective training, in whatever form it takes, touches the emotions. When employees begin to connect to the service initiative on an emotional level, that's when the pride factor kicks in. It is also when employees *become* the service initiative, not the spectators of it.

Service Improvement Team Action Steps

- Develop the education plan.
- Identify trainers, training materials, and training facilities.

- Ensure that all employees attend training regarding the service initiative.
- Conduct training sessions that are tailored to the specific needs of customer facing and support areas.
- Conduct training sessions for the executive team first, followed by management, followed by frontline employees. This helps to ensure that each organizational level is prepared to coach their employees. Adapt the training agendas provided in this chapter.
- Include specific "to do's" during the training, as well as action planning time.
- Ensure all managers know it is their responsibility to reinforce the training in their departments.
- Make the training sessions fun and interactive.
- Make customer service a significant part of new-hire orientation.
- Select only role model employees as on-the-job trainers.
- Ensure that *all* training includes links to customer service.

Pitfalls to Avoid

- Don't shortchange the length of the training sessions, even though some may push for "overviews."
- Don't present the service initiative as cast in stone. Let participants know that input and suggestions are welcome.
- Don't gloss over the difficulties of implementing the service behaviors. Be honest in admitting that excellence is hard work!
- Don't assume that participants are coming to the training with a blank slate. Recognize their experience.
- Don't think of customer service training as a standalone. It must be part of an integrated improvement strategy.

Chapter Seven

INTERVIEWING AND SELECTION

When dealing with unfriendly service employees, do you ever wonder how they got their jobs? The answer is that these employees were able to "fog the mirror" during the job interview. Some managers actually admit that they're just looking for warm bodies to fill open positions, and they usually get what they are looking for—warm bodies (with cold attitudes).

The old paradigm of simply hiring someone to fill a job is grossly inadequate in today's competitive environment. With customers viewing most products and services as commodities, the quality of a business's employees (including those who are at arm's length from the end customer, such as support personnel) is today's competitive advantage or disadvantage. No longer is technical skill the only requirement for job effectiveness. Soft skills, such as empathy, customer focus, communication, persuasiveness, listening, and many other qualities, are critical for success. It's the difference between the tasks it takes to be technically competent, and the characteristics it takes to be outstanding. Hiring the right people has taken on unprecedented importance.

The cost of poor hiring is staggering: One-and-one-half times annual salary is the number we see cited most frequently. This figure takes into account most of the direct turnover costs such as:

- recruiting/interviewing/testing to fill the open position
- overtime to cover the open position
- training the new person
- termination costs

When it comes to managerial mis-hires, the situation becomes even grimmer. Recruitment and hiring guru Brad Smart takes the factors above and includes items such as missed business opportunities, mistakes, and other failures and estimates the cost of a managerial mis-hire to be 24 times the manager's base salary! That's a number that should get anyone's attention.

This chapter covers methods for attracting and hiring service-oriented employees. Let's first point out that if you don't offer competitive pay and benefits, please stop and re-evaluate your compensation strategy. Money isn't everything and only motivates to a certain degree. But money is important. Your company doesn't have to be at the top of the compensation list to attract great people, but it sure helps to be near the top for similar jobs. When you make $10/hr, 50-cents/hr represents a 5 percent difference in pay. To many people, that 5 percent represents the ability to pay the rent or not. Don't kid yourself into thinking that your excellent company culture makes up for being evicted. It doesn't.

Anytime you are dealing with the recruiting and interviewing process, it's important to validate the process with your legal department or advisors. This chapter does not delve into the legalities of hiring. Although these principles will pass the legal test, be sure to review your hiring process with the lawyers.

Also, if your organization uses outside recruiters or head-hunters for filling certain positions, the principles in this chapter apply. The clearer your expectations are for the recruiters you contract, the greater the likelihood you'll get candidates who are suited for your company's culture. Don't turn the reins over to outside recruiters—ultimate responsibility for hiring should still reside with the hiring manager.

What Are You Looking For?

Every job requires a special blend of skills and talents if the job is to be done masterfully. At the Starbucks near Dennis's home, one of the baristas epitomizes the concept of right-fit talent. While all of the baristas do a fine job, James stands out through his uncanny knowledge of customer names and their favorite beverages. While Starbucks emphasizes this in their training, James takes it way beyond what can be trained. He prepares beverages for customers even before they walk in the door, having seen them walking in from the parking lot. He knows the names of customers' family members and keeps up a running banter even when it's busy, including just about everyone in the discussion. Talk about right-fit talent.

There are bad, average, and outstanding coffee shop employees, engineers, dentists, accountants, custodians, and presidents. The outstanding ones not only possess the necessary skills for their jobs, they appear to be born for their roles. Excellence seems to come naturally to these individuals, and everyone around them can see that someone special is at work. The trick is to discover the qualities of these special performers and find other people just like them. Unfortunately, these special qualities are different for every job and for every company's culture, so you can't simply develop a single set of job criteria and apply those criteria to any position. Through observation and analysis, however, you can discover the unique talents possessed by outstanding performers in a particular role.

Talent Is King

Every job requires a unique set of skills, knowledge, and talents. According to the Gallup organization—and as outlined in their book, *First, Break All the Rules* (authored by Marcus Buckingham and Curt Coffman)—talent is king. *Talents*, as described by Gallup, are the way in which a person looks at the world—recurring patterns of thought, feeling, or behavior. Talents define what drives a person and how he or she thinks and relates with others. While skills can be trained and knowledge can be taught, a person's talents are pretty well ingrained by the teen years. Whereas a person's talents can evolve and grow, their talents are not likely to *change*. Yes, there could be some life-altering occurrence that causes a complete change in a person, but even then the person's underlying talents are likely to still be there.

For example, if someone doesn't have a talent for noticing and paying attention to details, an important talent for an accountant, sending him to a great training class is not going to magically make this person detail-oriented. He may improve a bit, but suddenly becoming a star performer is not likely. Send an accountant who has the talent for attention to detail to a great training class, and this person gets excited, participates, learns some new skills to enhance his talent, and becomes even more valuable on the job.

Uncovering the Talents Required for Excellent Performance

Okay, so you've got an opening for a specific job. You probably can list the skills the job requires, such as the ability to operate a computer or cash register, lift 50 pounds, write computer code, and the other technical elements necessary for the position. But how do you discover the *talents* necessary to do an *outstanding* job? The answer is to observe and talk with people who are already performing that job in an outstanding manner. Watch them work and compare their performance to that of mediocre or average performers. What is different? Look beyond the basic mechanics of the job.

In a grocery store, for instance, you may notice that average stockers simply put items on a shelf and move on. You notice that your superstars, however, take a moment to step back and see how everything looks before moving on. The superstars may make small adjustments to the display before starting the next task. All this will probably happen very quickly and even unconsciously. Common sense tells you that superstar stockers must take more time to do the job, but you notice it actually takes superstars *less* time to do the job. Observing further, you notice that average stockers simply pile products on their carts before wheeling the carts out to the store floor. Your superstars, however, not only seem to get more on the carts, they have the items in a particular order. It didn't take them more time to do this because it comes to them naturally. These superstars have a talent for attention to detail and a talent for organization. If you want a team of outstanding stockers, you'd better find people who love the details and love to organize things.

Analyzing Behaviors

So you've observed the behaviors that separate your superstar employees from the average ones. Now you must determine the unique talents that cause excellent job performance so that you can discover whether a job applicant possesses the appropriate talents. After observing the behavioral differences of your excellent versus average performers, you must dig deeper to find out the talent reasons for the differences. The best way to dig deeper is through a question-and-answer process based on your observations. Ask a series of questions, such as those shown in Figure 7.1, of your outstanding and average performers and seek out those questions answered differently by your superstars. You'll be looking for themes that your superstars seem to consistently bring out that your average performers do not. Continuing with the grocery stocker, for example, you might ask, "When do you consider a shelf stocked?" From your average performers you may hear similar themes such as, "When the spaces are filled." From superstars you may hear, "When the shelf looks appealing," or "I know when everything looks right, the spaces are filled, the labels all face the same way, everything looks to be in the right place." You notice from the superstar responses that there's a desire to make sure everything *looks* right, not just a desire to put items on the shelves.

Part of your job in interviewing applicants, then, is to determine if the applicant has a desire to make things look right. Let's say, for example, a job applicant had previous experience working at a fast-food restaurant. You might ask, "How did you decide when an order was ready for the customer?" Your potential superstars will answer that, not only were all of the food items there, but also that everything looked good on the tray before giving it to the customer. Are there many fast-food employees that actually make sure things look good? No. That's the point. You want to find those talented few who are wired to make sure that things look right.

Keep in mind that the list of questions in Figure 7.1 is provided as a thought starter for meeting one-on-one with some of your employees to begin uncovering superstar talents. You'll have to

---

- What part of this job is most rewarding for you?
- When you are a customer, what does great service look like to you?
- What tools are of greatest help to you in doing your job?
- What do you think is expected of you as an employee?
- What do you think it takes to be considered *great* at your job?
- What do you find most frustrating about serving our customers?
- What does a leader do to get your best performance?
- What makes you feel successful at your job?
- How do you get everything done that needs to be done in your job?
- What frustrates *you* as a customer?
- What factors need to be in place to motivate you to do your *best* work?
- What is the best part about serving our customers?
- What role do fellow employees play in your satisfaction at work?
- How would you describe excellent performance in a job such as yours?
- Why is your role important to the organization?

Figure 7.1 Sample Talent Questions for Current Employees (Go to www.UnleashingExcellence.com to download a customizable copy of this form.)

customize the questions to match the job. We can't provide the correct answers to the questions because it depends upon the job as well as the culture of your organization. Remember, you're looking for those questions that your superstars answer differently than average performers.

What themes appear in the answers of great employees? After meeting with a number of outstanding and average performers, you may find that the two groups answer only three to four questions differently. That's okay. These become your magic interview questions. Obviously, you'll be asking other questions, but these few questions are the ones that will offer real insight into what makes the applicant tick and if they are at least likely to be superstar performers.

Armed with information about the qualities of your strongest current performers in a particular role, you then create an interview guide to be used whenever interviewing applicants for a position in that role. The interview guide should include not only the questions to ask, but also the themes the interviewer should listen for, based on the themes highlighted by your current superstars.

First Financial Bankshares, introduced in Chapter 5, created interview guides for each of the major positions in the organization. With additional assistance from the Bartlett Group, a consulting firm that specializes in creating job profiles and performance management tools, First Financial Bankshares has developed a process that has produced outstanding results. Under their new format for interviewing prospective tellers, for example, applicants first complete an online application and, if qualified, the applicant will then go through a telephone interview with the hiring manager using the behavioral interview tool they've developed. If the hiring manager decides the applicant is qualified to continue in the process, a face-to-face interview is scheduled, continuing with behavior-based questions. Human Resources is involved throughout and assists with the final selection based on all of the data collected throughout the interview process. Leo Bartlett, founder of the Bartlett Group, told us:

"To meet the customer's expectations, we must capture the behaviors of top-performing tellers, as an example, when 'they *are doing their job*,' and create a Benchmark Job Profile. The Job Profile includes the competencies and key behaviors of a particular position when those service behaviors are exceeding the customer's expectations. These are then used in the selection process, training of new employees, and coaching new and existing employees toward top performance."

According to Gary Gragg, First Financial Bankshare's co-champion of the Interviewing and Selection Leadership Action, all of this takes time. "But we don't apologize for taking a long time to make the selection," says Gragg. "We know how important it is to hire the right person."

Figure 7.2 shows a portion of the interview guide First Financial Bankshares uses for interviewing potential tellers. Note the structure of the document—it not only provides the themes for the interviewer to listen for, but it also provides a rating scale for the quality of the applicant's response. The structure of the interview guide ensures thoroughness and consistency in the interview process and also creates a tool for evaluating candidates when it comes time to make the selection.

Question: Tell me about the most rewarding part of your last job.
Response: _____

_____

_____

_____

Listen for examples when they used their behaviors to:
- Get satisfaction from working with and helping customers
- Making customers happy
- Develop strong personal relationships with customers
- Receive customer compliments on their service

Figure 7.2 Sample Interview Guide (Bank Teller Position)
Reprinted with permission of First Financial Bankshares and the Bartlett Group.

Strength of Candidate's Responses:	Rating Scale:
1 2 3 4 5 Situation Specifics	1 – Very Weak
1 2 3 4 5 Detailed Behaviors Used	2 – Weak
1 2 3 4 5 Recent Example (within last 6 months)	3 – Neither Weak nor Strong
1 2 3 4 5 Frequency of Behavior	4 – Strong
1 2 3 4 5 Able to Give Reference Support	5 – Very Strong

Question: Give me an example of a time when you thought you were "great" at your job. What was the job and what specifically did you do that made you feel great?

Response: _____

_____

_____

_____

Listen for behaviors that describe being "great" such as:
- Going the extra mile to satisfy the customers needs
- Being efficient, accurate and consistent
- Having the knowledge to solve customer issues
- Developing trust and relationships
- Being personable, friendly, outgoing with customers
- Calling customers by their name

Strength of Candidate's Responses:	Rating Scale:
1 2 3 4 5 Situation Specifics	1 – Very Weak
1 2 3 4 5 Detailed Behaviors Used	2 – Weak
1 2 3 4 5 Recent Example (within last 6 months)	3 – Neither Weak nor Strong
1 2 3 4 5 Frequency of Behavior	4 – Strong
1 2 3 4 5 Able to Give Reference Support	5 – Very Strong

NOTE: The actual interview guide consists of twelve questions.

Figure 7.2 (*Continued*)

If you don't want to go it alone, there are plenty of organizations that can assist with this process. As already mentioned, the Bartlett Group, using the Drake P3 Profile Tool, assisted First Financial Bankshares in developing their behavioral interviewing tool. Other firms such as Profiles International, Predictive Index, and Gallup can also assist.

Great People: Where Do You Find Them?

A common lament we hear is, "But we can't find qualified (insert job title)!" And yet, organizations in the same or similar industries seem to find outstanding employees from the same labor pool as those organizations that complain about the lack of qualified applicants. The difference is that successful organizations treat recruiting and hiring as a critical success factor that requires the same ongoing attention as product innovation, financial planning, or strategy formation.

You should always be recruiting. Even if you don't have an immediate job opening, you should still be recruiting. Too many companies wait until they are desperate for help before they begin looking and end up settling for "warm bodies." This is a recipe for mediocre service performance. Admittedly, you probably won't actually hire people when you don't have openings, but you're building a database of potential hires for when an opening does occur. So, where do you find great people?

Your Current Great People

You've already identified your outstanding customer service performers through the talent analysis discussed earlier. Ask your superstars for help in finding superstars because the likelihood is that these employees know people just like themselves. High performers typically recommend high performers because they can't stand working around mediocre performers.

Other Companies' Great People

Always be prepared to hand out your business card for those times you receive great service from someone in a position similar to one in your own organization. Don't look at this as stealing great people. Okay, it is stealing great people. But, if the person is happy in his or her job, he or she's not going to change companies anyway. If the person is unhappy in his or her job, you've done a good deed. You can also ask this wonderful service person if he or she knows anyone just like him or her who may be looking.

An attendee in one of our customer service workshops put this idea to work soon after the workshop. As vice president of a collections department, she acknowledged that finding good collectors was a challenge. After hearing our suggestion of giving your business card to outstanding service providers, she did just that to fill an open position in her operation. An employee of Taco Bell demonstrated outstanding people skills, and the VP offered her business card, inviting the employee to give her a call if she had interest in a position. The Taco Bell employee did call, interviewed, got the job, and turned out to be the perfect pick for the position.

Another source of potentially great people is any organization that may be going out of business or going through layoffs. Contrary to popular myth, good people do get laid off. Most companies want good things to happen to their good people. Take the time to meet with HR representatives of those closing or downsizing companies and ask for recommendations. You might worry about companies dumping less than stellar performers, but remember, you're simply looking for potentially great people to interview. You'll still put these individuals through a rigorous interview process.

Employee Scouting Programs

More and more companies are implementing scouting programs in which a "bounty" is offered to current employees for referring potential new hires. These programs offer an incentive such as

$500 for such referrals—typically half the amount when the applicant is hired and the other half when the person completes 90 days on the job. We would recommend that the entire incentive not only be contingent upon the applicant completing the 90-day employment period, but also achieving a determined performance threshold based on a comprehensive 90-day performance evaluation. You want *great* people, not just warm bodies that someone recommends to collect the bounty. Again, be sure to consult your legal department regarding compliance issues.

While we feel that scouting programs are effective and should be part of your recruiting toolkit, remember that your current superstar employees are your best source for potential future superstars. Talk to your current great people personally.

Job Fairs and Open House Events

Job fairs and open house events provide wonderful opportunities to seek out potentially excellent employees. You get to see applicants interact with each other as well as with members of your organization. You can also interview a lot of applicants in a relatively short time. Of course, in a job fair environment you're competing with other organizations for the same group of potential applicants, but the dynamics of a busy job fair can help you see how applicants perform under pressure. An open house hosted by your company allows you to design the entire experience. Here are a couple of elements to consider when designing an open house (or even a job fair booth):

1. Ensure that the atmosphere of the open house models that of your company. If you are a fun, wacky company, the event should be fun and wacky. If you are a traditional, formal organization (which is okay, by the way), your event should reflect traditional and formal attributes. If you say your company values *respect for the individual*, then treating open house attendees as cattle to be herded through a series of interviews flies directly in the face of what you say you value. Think everything through so that all aspects of the event

communicate your culture. In fact, we suggest Service Mapping (discussed in Chapter 4) the open house from start to finish, through the lens of the attendees, so that you ensure the event models your culture down to the smallest detail.

2. Carefully observe the behaviors of job fair or open house attendees. Build some mingling time into the schedule before the program begins. Remember, you're looking for service-oriented people. Note those attendees who naturally start conversations, laugh easily, and seem to put others at ease. Who offers to get another attendee a snack from the snack table? Also note those individuals who keep to themselves, avoid conversation, or seem uncomfortable interacting with people they don't know. If you're looking for people who naturally engage with your customers, you've just gotten a snapshot of the future.

The Interview

Anyone who has conducted job interviews knows that they are hard to do. We've all made the mistake of scheduling several interviews one after another and gone home that evening brain dead, not remembering who said what, much less whether any of the applicants were right for the job. Our hats are off to those who interview others for a living; they are special people.

The direct manager of the open position should be the primary interviewer. Others may participate, especially in any kind of initial screening, but the manager of the open position should interview the final candidates. The manager has a vested interest in selecting the right person. Also, by conducting the final interviews, the manager will learn a lot about the person eventually selected, thereby setting the foundation for a strong relationship. Finally, it is generally agreed by the experts that the most important function of any leader is to hire the right person for the right job.

Preparation for the Interview

The primary tool used during the interview is the behavioral interview guide discussed earlier in the chapter. Again, every organization is different and will have to adapt the guide to their own situation, but using an interview guide eliminates a lot of the ambiguity associated with most interviews. Recognize that conducting an effective interview takes time, as well it should. You want to make sure you choose the *best* candidate, not the one who just happens to be good at interviewing. Many managers feel that they can interview someone in 15 to 20 minutes. That may be so, but we're willing to bet that those same managers have had a large share of mis-hires. An experienced, charismatic interviewee can be pretty convincing for 20 minutes. On the other hand, when an interview covers a variety of topics in depth, it's a little harder to maintain a façade. You can pick up on potential inconsistencies in responses and gain valuable insight from the applicant's behaviors throughout the process.

Figure 7.3 provides some sample questions to ask about *every* job the applicant has held. Going back several years may seem wasteful, but remember; talents are usually lasting. You want to see a pattern of behavior, performance, likes, dislikes, and challenges over time. This way you can understand what truly makes the person tick and, more importantly, if what makes the interviewee tick is similar to your current superstars. The old interview saying is true: Past performance is your best indicator of future performance. You'll notice that the questions in Figure 7.3 do not directly address customer service. We suggest that you see if the *applicant* brings up the customer service aspects of the job. If he or she doesn't, then you can ask specific customer service questions adapted from Figure 7.1. But, if the applicant is really wired for service, his or her answers to these questions should contain customer-related themes. And, to be predictive of success on the job, these themes should be similar to those of your current service superstars.

Note that, for each job the interviewee has had, you ask for specific references. Brad Smart, in his book *Top Grading*, strongly

The following questions should be asked about *every position* the applicant has held, beginning with his/her first job and progressing forward. These questions are designed to highlight the applicant's focus (or lack of focus) on customer service. Added to the questions below will be the talent questions chosen from Figure 7.1. You will, of course, also need to include questions regarding specific skills required for the job.

As the applicant responds to each question below, listen carefully to the focus of the response. Does the applicant focus on the customer service aspects of the job? Are you hearing some of the same themes you heard from your current superstars?

- What were your responsibilities in this job?
- What did you find most enjoyable about the job?
- What did you find least enjoyable about the job?
- What did you learn from the job that may help you in the position you are applying for?
- Tell me about a specific story or occurrence regarding the job that you are particularly proud of.
- Who was your direct supervisor?
    - May we contact him?
    - How can we contact him?*
- What do you feel your immediate supervisor will indicate as your major strengths?
- What do you feel your immediate supervisor will indicate as possible weaknesses?

*If possible, have the applicant arrange the contact. The likelihood of speaking with the direct supervisor is increased if the applicant makes the arrangements.

Figure 7.3   Customer Service–Related Interview Questions (Go to www. UnleashingExcellence.com to download a customizable copy of this form.)

advocates what he calls the TORC principle, which stands for Threat Of Reference Check. You want the applicant to know that you definitely plan to conduct reference checks, so he or she may as well tell you what his or her previous boss will say about his or her performance. Smart also recommends that you have the interviewee make the arrangements for contacting the references. This helps avoid the problem of the reference simply passing you off to Human Resources, which will only provide the dates of employment, if that.

We know that you may be thinking, "Well, if the applicant arranges for the reference contact, won't she ask for a good recommendation?" Probably. But you will have very thorough information from your interview and will also be asking in-depth questions of the reference. You'll see if the information matches up or if there are inconsistencies. Also, having conducted many reference checks in the past (and been a reference ourselves), you can tell when a former boss is dancing around a question. When you ask a reference, "Tell me about the quality of Sally's work," and you get responses such as, "She always worked hard," or "Sally took great pride in her work," and you never really get an answer about the *quality* of Sally's work, well, you've gotten your answer. You know it, the reference knows it, and he or she will never have to admit to anything less than a glowing recommendation.

Conducting the Interview

There are hundreds of interviewing books that can provide basic interviewing guidelines. The basics are important, such as the interviewer being on time, holding phone calls, and reviewing the applicant's resume in advance. There are several other important actions, however, that help ensure that you select service-oriented employees.

The Interview Atmosphere and Setting

Earlier in this chapter we mentioned modeling your company's values during job fairs and open houses. This same rule holds true for any interview. Everything speaks! If you say that your organization pays attention to detail, then the interview environment should reflect that value. If one of your core values is creativity, the interview environment should communicate that value.

We once worked with a major petroleum company on a service improvement strategy. While touring gas stations and convenience stores one day, we noticed a store entrance that was in poor shape and had trash everywhere. The company representative who was hosting us was mortified and exclaimed, "Can you believe this?" Yes, we could believe what we were seeing. When we entered the store there was a job interview taking place. Unfortunately, the interview was taking place in a dirty broom closet, and the interviewer and applicant were both sitting on overturned mop buckets. Everything speaks, and the interview environment was loudly communicating that attention to detail was not part of the store's culture.

Walt Disney World, as well as the other Disney theme parks, has taken the idea of the interview experience to an entirely new level. In fact, they call interviewing "casting for a role in the show" because they want applicants to understand that the job is bigger than the tasks associated with any particular job. "Cast members" are part of a show and therefore must be chosen carefully for a role in that show. The Casting Center (interview office) is a specially designed building that reflects the Disney culture down to the smallest detail. Experiencing the Casting Center has the feel of experiencing a Disney attraction. To enter the building, for example, the applicant turns a large brass nose from an *Alice in Wonderland* character. Upon entering, the applicant is surrounded by gilded statuettes of Disney characters and murals presenting whimsical Disney themes. Anyone visiting the Casting Center immediately knows that this will be no ordinary interview; it will be an experience. Just like a visit to Walt Disney World. After signing in with the receptionist (who treats the applicant as a welcome guest), groups of applicants watch a 12-minute film that explains what it's like to work at Disney, as well as the job requirements to be considered for a position. The film clearly describes what they call PATA, which stands for Pay, Availability, Transportation, and Appearance. While the film is produced in typical Disney entertaining fashion, none of the items discussed are presented as "suggestions"; they're presented as nonnegotiables. It's important to manage the expectations of Disney job applicants, since most have visited the theme parks as guests and might be expecting a Disney job to be all fun and games. So effective is the film in managing expectations that Disney has found that roughly 15 percent of applicants screen themselves out before even meeting with an interviewer.

We sometimes get pushback from companies regarding this concept. Management indignantly states that they have no place to conduct interviews that would be of the quality that truly represents the company's service philosophy. Our response is that, if you want to build a world-class service culture, you've got to create such an environment. No, it's not easy. If it were easy, every company would do it. The best will. Be creative about providing a suitable environment, recognizing that creative doesn't necessarily mean expensive.

By the way, the "everything speaks" concept applies to anything connected with the interview process. Prescreening tests, the jobs section of your company's web site, and the postings on the various Internet job search sites all convey a message about your organization. Make sure that the details convey the right message.

Observe the Applicant's Behavior Before the Interview

Actions speak much louder than words. In their book *Nuts! Southwest Airline's Crazy Recipe for Business and Personal Success,* Kevin and Jackie Freiberg tell the story of a highly decorated ex-military pilot applying for a pilot job at Southwest Airlines. From an experience and technical perspective, this applicant was supremely qualified. Yet, as he traveled to Dallas for his interview (on a Southwest plane), this applicant was rude to a ticket agent and was then arrogant with the receptionist. Needless to say, he didn't get the job. Southwest Airlines isn't just looking for excellent pilots. They are looking for excellent pilots with excellent people skills.

Plan for colleagues to greet the applicant as you observe the interaction. Does the applicant seem quick to engage with others or does he or she give quick, one-word answers, preferring to wait quietly for the interview. Admittedly, the applicant may be nervous, but this lack of engagement should at least raise a warning flag. If you are looking for outgoing, friendly employees, you should expect to see these qualities in their behavior.

When you eventually hire the right person, how much of their time will be spent on the phone? We're constantly amazed at the number of call centers, for example, that don't conduct any of their interviews over the phone. The only contact customers have with these employees is via telephone, yet the company has no idea how applicants present themselves on the telephone. If the job entails a lot of phone work, spend at least some time talking with the applicant on the phone. Does the applicant sound the way you want excellent employees to sound? Or does the applicant sound monotone and, well, boring? You may think, "We can send the person to a telephone etiquette class for training." Chances are, the applicant has been talking on the phone several times a day since he or she was 10 years old. If he or she has averaged just three phone calls per day and is 25 years old, the applicant has participated in 16,425 calls. Most telephone etiquette classes contain *two* role-plays. The odds are stacked against lasting improvement. Go with what you hear.

Carefully review the applicant's resume as well as the job application. Highlight specific areas you'd like to discuss further in order to learn more about the talents the person had to apply to be successful in those areas. Review the resume for completeness and accuracy. If you're hiring someone for a job that requires "attention to detail," a sloppy resume should certainly raise a red flag.

The Interview Itself

During the actual interview, you'll guide the discussion through the applicant's experience while focusing on the talents needed to do the job well. Remember, you're listening for themes and patterns. Even if the applicant has little work experience due to young age, you can still dig into school experiences, community work, and other information while following the same basic questioning pattern as noted in Figure 7.3. You want to get as much information as possible so that you can validate the consistency of answers.

The magic opening to an interview question is: "Tell me about a time when . . ." This type of question allows the applicant to reveal whether or not a pattern of behavior is truly a part of his or her makeup. Let's say, for instance, the job entails the talent of reading the emotions of customers in order to truly understand and solve their problems. You might ask: "Tell me about a time when you had to do some digging to get to the customer's real problem." Some guidelines for evaluating responses include:

- Does the applicant provide *specific* examples? You want the applicant to respond with an actual occurrence that you can probe for deeper understanding of what actually happened. When, on the other hand, an applicant responds, "Well, I usually try to . . . ," it may mean that he or she doesn't have a specific example. Ask again for an example. If the responses are consistently vague, the likelihood is that "reading emotions" is not a talent the applicant possesses.
- Do the applicant's responses align with the responses of your current superstars to similar questions? The answers won't be exact duplicates, but do the same themes appear? Does the applicant talk about listening to the customer's tone of voice and reading the customer's body language just like your superstars did?
- Are the responses consistent? In the course of the interview, you'll be asking about various experiences that applicant has had, but the questions themselves will be the same. Do the responses seem consistent or are the answers all over the place? If there seems to be little consistency in responses to similar questions, the person is probably making up the answers.

Be sure not to telegraph the answers or themes you're looking for. While this may seem obvious, telegraphing is done all the time because it's such an easy trap to fall into. Here's a typical example: "We're pretty high volume around here. Tell me about your ability to handle multiple priorities while still giving customers your full attention." Applicants know pretty clearly the direction their response should take. Instead, by asking, "When it's busy, how do you get everything done that needs to be done?" you're able to listen for a response that includes still giving customers full attention, without cueing the applicant on the desired answer.

A good rule of thumb in interviewing is for the interviewer to talk only about 20 percent of the time. The only way to really get to the essence of an applicant's qualifications is to listen carefully and use your talk time primarily to ask probing questions. Being comfortable with silence after asking a question takes some getting used to, but it's important. Interviewers are often too quick to jump in when there's an uncomfortable silence, and stifle what could end up being a thoughtful response or a telling gap in the applicant's qualifications.

Be very observant during the interview. Remember, you're looking for service-oriented individuals. Behaviors to look for during an interview include:

- Does the applicant make appropriate eye contact? Or are his or her eyes constantly moving around to the point where you are wondering what he or she's looking for? We've all dealt with service providers who never really look at us.
- Does the applicant demonstrate appropriate enthusiasm? An applicant who can't be enthusiastic during an interview is unlikely to be enthusiastic 8 hours per day, 5 days per week. On the other hand, does the applicant exhaust you with enthusiasm? We've all dealt with service providers who are *too* enthusiastic, to the point of being irritating.
- Does the applicant smile often? If you're looking for friendly, approachable employees, you had better see that natural smile. Sound trivial? How many times have you thought, "It wouldn't hurt her to smile once in a while"?

- Does the applicant use positive, upbeat language? Do you feel engaged by what the applicant is saying? Or does the applicant use negative, downbeat language? The likelihood is that this is how he or she will talk with fellow employees and customers.

Take plenty of notes throughout the interview. You should note the applicant's responses to key questions as well as your observations. A strong legal recommendation is to only record the facts as you hear and see them. For example, don't write, "The applicant seemed evasive." Instead, write, "The applicant did not provide specific examples." Don't write, "The applicant seemed shy." Instead, write, "The applicant provided short answers and didn't ask me any questions. He made little eye contact during the interview." As long as you write the facts only, not opinions, you should be okay legally if your notes are subpoenaed for some reason. Again, ask your legal department for their advice on the subject.

Reference Checks

As discussed earlier in the chapter, we strongly recommend that you conduct thorough reference checks. Getting through to references is always a challenge. And, in today's litigious environment, many employers are reluctant to provide references at all. One suggestion is to contact references via phone versus email, since being asked to put information in writing may immediately shut down the reference. Pierre Mornell, in his book *Hiring Smart!*, presents a novel way for getting potential references to return your call. He suggests leaving a voicemail letting the person know that a job candidate has provided his or her name as a reference and that you'd like to discuss the person's qualifications. Then, Mornell says, conclude your message with, "Please call me back if the candidate was outstanding." Most references will return the call if the candidate is indeed excellent, not wanting to ruin the person's chances for the job. And, if no references call back, you've learned something without ever actually speaking with the references.

Figure 7.4 provides some questions to ask references. The purpose of the reference check is to ask a peer about the applicant's performance and to check the reference's responses against those

---

The following list of questions are meant to supplement current reference check questions that interviewers typically ask, such as employment dates, reason for termination, job responsibilities and skills, and quality of work. The questions are designed to uncover patterns of behavior regarding the applicant's customer service orientation.

- What did the applicant seem to find most enjoyable about the job?
- What did the applicant seem to find least enjoyable about the job?
- What words or phrases would you use to describe the applicant's ability to interact with customers? Explain.
- Describe how the applicant handled challenging customer situations.
- What did customers say about the applicant?
- What did you find motivated the applicant to perform at her best?
- What did you find to be the applicant's de-motivators?
- What should I know about the best way(s) to supervise the applicant?
- What words or phrases would you use to describe the applicant's interaction with other employees?
- Tell me about a time in which you had to coach the applicant. What was the impact on her performance?
- Would you recommend that I hire this person for the job that I've described to you?

NOTE: Some questions must be adjusted for those applicants in a support role, with little or no end-customer contact.

Figure 7.4 Reference Check Questions (Go to www.UnleashingExcellence.com to download a customizable copy of this form.)

of other references *and* the applicant. Discuss some of the responses the applicant offered during the interview. For example, you might say, "Dianne mentioned that you viewed her as a source of ideas for improving departmental processes." Leave it at that and let the reference either validate the response or hem and haw about how to best reply. Do consistent themes appear during your discussion with the reference, or do you get a different picture than you got from the applicant? The more you engage the reference in conversation, the greater the likelihood that he or she will overtly or unconsciously give you the information you need.

Interviewing Skills Training

It's surprising how many organizations offer no training to managers on effective interviewing skills. Along with the development of the interviewing tools and principles discussed in this chapter, it's vital to also provide training to those individuals who will be conducting interviews. The training should not only include the use of the tools described, but also how to conduct an effective interview. Included should be such topics as interviewing legalities, asking open-ended questions, listening skills, how to probe for deeper understanding, and observation skills. Being an effective interviewer is not easy, and training will help ensure that your interviewers are equipped with what they need to be successful.

Concluding Thoughts

Many organizations feel that the selection process is really about getting people hired, then sending them to a training class that will "fix" them so that they perform in a way that aligns with the organization's values. Of course this doesn't work. These organizations continue the revolving door process of hiring, training, firing, hiring, training, firing.

The purpose of this chapter is to help you locate and select service-oriented employees. The process recommended takes time and effort. The payoff, however, is that you are much more likely to hire individuals who are "wired" to provide excellent service, respond to the training you provide, and remain loyal to your organization. The extra effort will pay you back many times over.

Service Improvement Team Action Steps

Note: Some organizations may decide to use an outside consulting firm to assist with some of the following action steps.

- Determine which role or roles will be the initial subject(s) of the behavioral interview process. Ultimately, every position in the organization should be included.
- Observe and interview your best employees in order to uncover their service talents.
- Develop a structured, behavioral interview guide for each job position.
- Provide interview skills training for any individual responsible for interviewing.
- Develop multiple recruiting channels, with a strong focus on referrals from current superstar employees.
- Design all recruiting processes, as well as the interview process itself, so that the organization's culture and values are clearly modeled. Use Service Mapping to assist with this process.
- Track how the best employees were recruited to your company.
- Create and distribute a structured tool for conducting reference checks.
- Ensure the interviewing and selection tools are being used consistently.

Pitfalls to Avoid

- Don't wait until you have an opening to begin the recruiting process. You'll be in desperation mode.
- Don't wing it during the interview. Have a plan.
- Don't disregard the pre-interview behaviors of applicants. Such behaviors can be predictive.
- Don't rush the interview. Find out what makes the applicant tick.

Chapter Eight

MEASUREMENT

"Man, I sure did love my first car, a real classic. It looked awful, it was so banged up, but it ran great. Unfortunately, the gas gauge didn't work. It always showed FULL. All the other gauges worked, so I never over-heated the engine or anything like that. But I always had to guess how much gas I had left in the tank. Sometimes I was right; sometimes I was wrong. I kept an empty gas can in the trunk for the times I was wrong and had to walk to a gas station. I got rid of the car after getting stuck and missing class. I should have just fixed the gas gauge and kept the car. All I needed was to know when to go to the gas station."

S ervice improvement measurements are like the gauges on a car dashboard. A handful of measures can give you the data needed to keep going. Up to this point you've developed your service strategy, kicked off the initiative, trained your staff, and aligned your hiring process with your service culture. In this chapter we'll focus on measuring your customer service results.

Feedback from readers of the first edition of *Unleashing Excellence*, as well as comments from our consulting clients, suggested that Measurement is the most challenging of the Leadership Actions. If you've ever tried to measure customer service you know it can be a tricky job. Factories can measure defects, units produced, production efficiency, or hundreds of other factors. What do you measure in the service industry— smiles? The answer is sometimes yes. The culprit behind most of the struggles with this Leadership Action is that organizations try to overcomplicate things. Whereas measurement factors such as revenue, expenses, margins, and other typical business measurements tend to be very precise, customer service measurements can often be a bit subjective. Just how friendly was the restaurant server? Was the phone operator response timely and complete? It's hard to put a specific number on such opinions; therefore, organizations try to develop mind-numbing techniques for accurate quantification of customer service factors, or they abandon the measurement effort altogether because of the potential "softness" of the measurements.

Our approach to measurement in this book may be a little different than approaches you've seen before. Most books, on the topic of measuring customer satisfaction, focus on global, large-scale satisfaction surveys and their many variations. We'll touch on overall satisfaction surveys because they are important; but we will spend the bulk of this chapter focusing on local, day-to-day measurements. By "local" we mean localized to a department, workgroup, or job area. Our experience shows that local measures are highly effective in keeping employees engaged and focused on service improvement. Employees like to know how they are doing *right now*. Organization-wide, customer satisfaction measurements usually have a fairly long lead-time.

Even though our primary focus will be on local measurements, let's first take a look at your key business metrics and overall customer satisfaction measurements.

Key Business Metrics

The main purpose of initiating a service improvement initiative, of course, is to have a positive impact on your business results. So our first recommendation is to ask, "What business metrics are we hoping to influence?" Keep in mind that lots of dynamics influence business metrics. The state of the economy, actions of competitors, new regulations, new technologies, and a host of other factors impact business results. But that doesn't diminish the fact that the ultimate objective of your service initiative is to improve your business results.

Some top-level business metrics that should be affected by improvements in your customer service include:

- customer retention
- market share
- revenue
- employee turnover
- stock performance
- bond rating
- repeat purchase rate

Take a look at your top-level business metrics and decide which you will use as gauges of the overall success of the service initiative. Keep in mind that these metrics are usually slow to respond to internal initiatives, but you do want them to respond. Establish your baseline measurements and track your progress.

Customer Satisfaction Measurements

These measurements answer the question, "What do our customers think of us?" Anyone who has bought a new car has probably gotten a JD Powers survey. If you were a patient in a hospital, it's likely that 2 weeks or so after you returned home you got a survey in the mail. Customer satisfaction measurements give companies information that can be tracked over time and benchmarked internally and against other organizations.

We're going to give a strong recommendation right here: If you can, bring in professionals to help you with formal customer satisfaction measurements. There are many companies who specialize in surveying your customers and providing you with detailed reports.

The value of an organization-wide survey is that it can give you a detailed report of the different areas within the organization and how each is measuring up. Reports can come out quarterly or more frequently. Press Ganey Associates, a firm that specializes in measurement of hospitals and healthcare, can also track satisfaction scores daily using their Internet tool. The key is that the data are benchmarked against their massive database and can be compared to the data of similar-sized hospitals or specialties. The report gives an overall picture and also drills down to the department or unit level. They even provide a correlation analysis that highlights the service factors the hospital should focus on. The information is invaluable and can provide the foundation for ongoing service improvement. There are other companies that specialize in customer satisfaction surveys and we believe, if you have the budget, bringing in help is a wise investment. A professional firm should be able to customize the questions to get the information you need. Some cautions to be aware of, though:

- Too many surveys. How many times have you been barraged by companies seeking information about their service only to end up annoying you? Teri's pest-control company followed up their service visit with a phone call, a local office survey, then a company-wide survey! She felt like she had already given enough of her time to the first two surveys and resented the third intrusion.
- Too many questions. Try to keep the number of questions asked to a minimum. Lengthy surveys are a turn-off when you're asking someone to give you a moment of their time to do a "quick" survey.

- Not a good cross section of customers. Make sure that your survey company surveys a representative sample of your customer base and can provide reports that break down the results by category. And, since you're probably paying for it anyway, make sure the report breaks out the results of your most profitable customers since what may be issues to your least profitable and most profitable customers are very possibly not the same.
- Employees don't know how to take corrective action. Be sure to share the information with the people that need to know how to do something about it. Professional surveys may appear more like research versus simple feedback and that's where the data must be interpreted and translated for all levels to gain understanding of the issues.

Of course, the customer survey information is only useful if you *do* something with it; but more about that later.

What if We Don't Have Access to the Professionals?

What if you're a small organization where it doesn't make sense to bring in measurement professionals? You can still do formal customer satisfaction measurements. Lots of companies successfully use tools like focus groups, comment cards, mystery shoppers, and surveys developed in-house. There are also online survey tools such as 20/20 Insight GOLD and SurveyMonkey that allow you to create, distribute, and analyze your own surveys. You may not have the database professional firms use for benchmarking, but you can still collect meaningful information. What's important is that you have a baseline measurement from which you can track your progress. The sooner you establish these key indicators and begin measuring them, the sooner you will be able to see the progress of your service improvement efforts and show the value in what you are doing. Inevitably, someone from higher management is going to ask in a year or two, "So what have we gotten out of all of the effort on this service improvement process?" Make sure you don't change these key indicators over time; you may add to them, but to ensure consistency in the comparison of ratings you'll need to keep the same core measurements.

Figure 8.1 is an example of a survey you can tailor to your needs. We can hear the statisticians screaming that the questions have not been statistically analyzed for your particular industry and no correlation analysis has been done. They're right. But at least you will get some key information you need to make service decisions. And remember, that's the point.

1. Knowledge and skill of our employees:				
1	2	3	4	5
Extremely Poor	Poor	Average	Good	Excellent

Comments:

2. Availability of employees to help:				
1	2	3	4	5
Extremely Poor	Poor	Average	Good	Excellent

Comments:

3. Overall courtesy of employees:				
1	2	3	4	5
Extremely Poor	Poor	Average	Good	Excellent

Comments:

4. Ease of doing business with us:				
1	2	3	4	5
Extremely Poor	Poor	Average	Good	Excellent

Comments:

Figure 8.1 Sample Customer Survey (Go to www.UnleashingExcellence .com to download a customizable copy of this form.)

1	2	3	4	5

5. Overall rating of our company and its products/services:

1	2	3	4	5
Extremely Poor	Poor	Average	Good	Excellent

Comments:

6. Likelihood of doing business with us again:

1	2	3	4	5
Extremely Unlikely	Unlikely	Not Sure	Likely	Extremely Likely

Comments:

7. Likelihood that you would recommend us to others:

1	2	3	4	5
Extremely Unlikely	Unlikely	Not Sure	Likely	Extremely Likely

Comments:

Figure 8.1 (*Continued*)

There are three key questions in Figure 8.1. The others flesh out the information. The three key questions are:

- Overall, how satisfied are you with our product/service/ company?
- How likely are you to continue doing business with us?
- How likely are you to recommend us to others?

Likelihood to return and likelihood to recommend are considered key indicators of customer loyalty. Of course, if you can measure *actual* repeat business, and *actual* customer referrals, then do that. Those are the definitive satisfaction measurements!

Tailor the survey to your operation. If a department store decides to survey customers as they leave the store, it would be important to track what departments the customer visited. You would then ask questions 1 through 3 about each of those departments. A grocery store might do the same and have another section for the checkout line. An auto body shop could mail the survey to recent customers. If you're a small company, don't overcomplicate the process or you'll do the survey once and never again. Keep it simple—you'll get the information you need to improve the operation.

What Scores Matter

Notice the rating scale used in Figure 8.1. Most satisfaction surveys use a five- or seven-point scale, the highest ranking being along the lines of "Excellent." When (if) companies communicate survey results to their employees, they often combine the *Good* and *Excellent* responses into one percentage: "90 percent of customers surveyed rated us as good or excellent. Great work everyone!" Unfortunately, the 90 percent figure doesn't communicate that only 15 percent of the respondents rated themselves in the *Excellent* category. Studies have proven that only those customers who rate themselves as *Excellent* are truly loyal to your company. These studies show that customers rating *Good* defect to the competition as those who rate themselves as Neutral. If you eat at a local restaurant and it's good, you might return or you may just as likely eat somewhere else next time. If you eat at a local restaurant and it's *great*, it's likely that you *will* return and you'll probably recommend it to your friends. The "top box" is the only rating that counts in judging customer satisfaction.

Florida's Turnpike Enterprise, which consists of toll collectors, service plaza personnel, roadway service, highway patrol, road engineers, and so on, has made this distinction when it communicates two main measurements from their customer satisfaction survey to all personnel. The two measurements are: Satisfaction with Value for Toll Paid and Recommendation of the Turnpike System. The percent of Strongly Agree is separated out on both charts in comparison with the percent of Agree. See Figures 8.2 and 8.3 for examples of their charts.

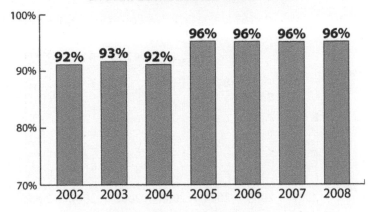

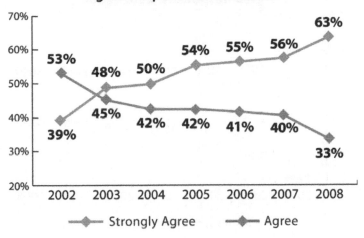

Figure 8.2 Recommendation of the Turnpike System

In Chapter 1, we mentioned the research of Fredrick Reich-held, which resulted in his groundbreaking book, *The Ultimate Question: Driving Good Profits and True Growth* (Harvard Business School Press, 2006). Reichheld's research has shown that one question can be most powerful in determining your loyal customers: How likely is it that you would recommend this

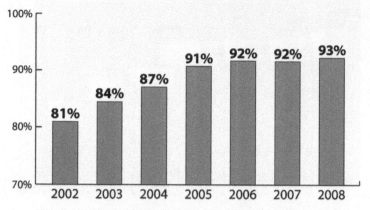

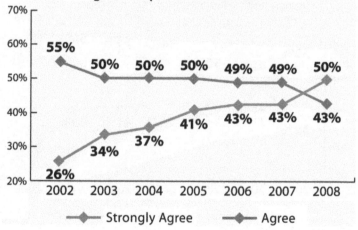

Figure 8.3 Value Received in the Form of Safety, Service, and Convenience

company to a friend or colleague? The metric that it produces is what Reichheld calls the Net Promoter Score (NPS), which has become an increasingly popular tool for measuring customer satisfaction. NPS is based on the premise that customers fall into three different categories: ''promoters,'' ''passives,'' and "detractors." On a survey scale of 1 to 10, *promoters* are those who respond with a rating of 9 or 10. These are your enthusiastic, loyal customers who keep coming back and are responsible for the bulk of referrals. *Passives* are those who respond with a rating of 7 or 8 on the survey scale. Passives are satisfied customers, but they aren't truly loyal to your organization—they may or may not do business with you again and may or may not recommend you to others. *Detractors* are those who respond with a rating of 1 to 6 on the scale. These are unhappy customers who may only be doing business with you because there is no other choice at the moment and, Reichheld says, are responsible for more than 80 percent of a company's negative word-of-mouth.

To grow your company in attracting and retaining customers, obviously you want as many promoters and as few detractors as possible. Reichheld's formula then is: $P - D = NPS$ (Promoters minus Detractors equals Net Promoter Score). Using this as a baseline measurement can help an organization track how they're perceived by customers and provide a foundation for strategizing improvement. We highly recommend Reichheld's book.

How you administer a customer satisfaction survey depends on your organization. You might decide to do a quarterly phone survey of your customers. You might do a mail out. Focus groups are effective because you can drill deeply into customer comments and get suggestions for improvement. Some companies ask customers if they have time to "answer a few questions" about their experience immediately following the experience (exit surveys). The important thing is to ask customers how you are doing. A few questions you may want to consider asking a focus group are:

- Given other options, why do you choose our company over our competitors?
  - Follow-up: In what aspects do you feel competitors perform well?
  - Follow-up: In what aspects do you feel competitors perform poorly?

- What are your top four or five expectations of our company?
- From your experience with our organization, what specific circumstances have resulted in your delight with our company?
- From your experience, what specific circumstances have resulted in recent customer frustration with our company?

Local Measurements

So far we've discussed formal, overall satisfaction measurements. These are important for taking the ongoing pulse of your customers. The questions asked on these surveys should be consistent so that results can be compared over time. You're creating your own benchmarks.

Another type of measurement is just as useful in advancing your service initiative. These are day-to-day, or local, measurements. They are less formal and are usually driven by a specific need or objective. They're helpful because they directly involve employees in the measurement *and* improvement processes.

An example shows how local measurements work. A resort hotel recently embarked on a service improvement effort. Every department committed to specific service behaviors that were based on the hotel's Service Standards. By participating in cross-departmental meetings, the Housekeeping department was surprised to hear Front Desk employees complain about Housekeeping's performance. Many guests were angry that their rooms weren't ready when they arrived to check in. Obviously, this was a major dissatisfier.

True, some guests arrived significantly before check-in time. But there were plenty of times that Housekeeping was simply behind on their work and rooms weren't ready at the published check-in time. Front Desk employees took a lot of grief from guests and resented the Housekeeping department because of it. Not a good environment for building a team.

Management could've easily demanded that Housekeepers speed up their work to alleviate guest dissatisfaction. The result, however, would've been:

- demoralized Housekeepers (they were doing their best with the processes that were in place).
- resentment between Front Desk employees and House-keepers.
- guests who continued to be frustrated because the rooms would not be cleaned faster despite management's demands.

Instead of making demands, Housekeeping management decided to enlist the help of the Front Desk and Housekeeping teams in measuring how many rooms were left unclean by check-in time. Housekeepers would then note why any rooms were not completed. By conducting this local measurement, they found that interruptions from the Housekeeping office were the main reason for getting behind. Most of the interruptions were to fulfill special guest requests. *Now* the team had something to work with.

Armed with the new information, the Housekeeping office started measuring what the special requests were for. After 1 week the team got together to review the data. By far the biggest culprit of delays was special requests for extra towels in guest rooms. They quickly figured the cost of permanently adding two extra towels per room versus the cost of fulfilling special requests for towels. The solution was to buy the extra towels. Guests were happy, Front Desk employees were happy, and the Housekeepers were proud of coming up with the solution.

As you read this story, you may have thought that the hotel's problem seemed simple and the solution was obvious. But it wasn't simple or obvious. There could've been hundreds of reasons why guest rooms weren't ready in time. Only by focusing on improving service, getting the right people involved, measuring performance, and *acting* on the information could the problem be solved with confidence.

Keys to Local Measurement Success

Local measurements should be linked to the overall service improvement effort.

The power of local service measures is that they're selected and managed by each workgroup. That doesn't mean, however, that the measurements should be random and disconnected. Every department or business unit should choose measures that directly link to the Service Philosophy and Service Standards. This brings some consistency to the effort. The Service Improvement Team can guide the company through the measurement process and make certain that different areas of the company aren't going in random directions.

The workgroup should be able to impact the factors they measure.

This principle seems like a no-brainer, but it's violated all the time. Imagine asking department store salespeople to measure customer comments and complaints about the mall's parking lot. The information might be useful, but the salespeople have no control over the parking lot. The store should figure out a better way for collecting that information. Salespeople *can* impact product returns, wait times, shelf stocking, and so on. It's much better for them to measure these areas because they can take direct action to improve the results.

The act of measuring shouldn't negatively impact the customer experience.

Most of us have been in the position of being "over measured." In some businesses it seems that every time you turn around someone is there with a clipboard asking questions. You've probably experienced restaurants where three employees in three minutes ask you how everything is. You probably want to say that everything would be great if they'd leave you alone so you could eat! If the customer is annoyed by the measurement system, something is wrong.

Improvement in one service factor shouldn't negatively impact another service factor.

The classic example of unintended consequences is the call center that measures the number and length of calls handled by each employee. The service factor they're probably trying to improve is customer wait time in the call queue—a valid goal. However, in the quest to shorten wait time, it's essential that customers don't feel rushed *during* the call.

"Our manager was really getting on us for call volume. Everything was about calls per hour. Every day she posted our individual call rates on the office wall. She verbally beat us up if we missed our goal. After a while, most of us figured out how to beat the system. If a call was going too long, some of us would 'accidentally' disconnect the customer so he had to call back. That way we could maintain a good call volume."

In the case of this call center, improving one service factor hurt another factor. The objective should have been to reduce wait times *without sacrificing call quality.* Involving employees in deciding local measurements can eliminate situations like this.

Deciding What to Measure

As you board a plane, have you ever looked in the cockpit? The number of gauges, switches, and levers is overwhelming. How does the pilot keep track of everything? During flight, there are four key gauges that the pilot focuses on. The gauges that tell: How fast are we going? How high are we? How much fuel do we have left? And in what direction are we heading? The other instruments are used for preflight checks and to help if there is a problem. The hardest part of local measurement is deciding what's important to measure and track.

Every area of the company should ask, "Who are our customers and what is important to them?" Service Maps developed by each team can be an excellent place to start. Since Service Maps shed light on how customers interact with the workgroup, it makes sense to use them as a measurement generator. What areas of opportunity did the Service Mapping process highlight?

Figure 8.4 provides some guidelines in deciding what to measure. It takes two dynamics into account: potential impact on the customer experience and the amount of control the team has over the service factor.

As you brainstorm possible measurements, plot them on the graph. The most effective measurements will be the ones that fall in the high impact, high influence quadrant. There will be disagreements over impact and influence, but that's part of the point—open dialogue is critical to ongoing improvement. Examples of local measurements we've seen used include:

- Physician's office wait schedule. Physicians' offices are notorious for running behind schedule. Who hasn't sat in a doctor's office fuming because it was clear that the staff

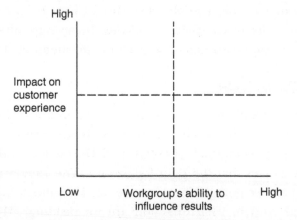

Figure 8.4 Deciding What to Measure (Go to www.UnleashingExcellence.com to download a customizable copy of this form.)

felt the doctor's time was more important than yours? In fact, more and more patients are changing doctors because of unacceptable waits. One office was determined to improve the situation without compromising the quality of patient–doctor face-time. They estimated that patients would be extremely satisfied if seen within 5 minutes of their appointment time (most of us would be thrilled to be seen within the hour!). The entire office team collaborated on measuring and improving performance. One thing they discovered was that, if patients with particular needs were scheduled first thing in the morning, the rest of the day could be scheduled and run efficiently. Most of these patients were happy to be the first of the day. The few that didn't want the early schedule were accommodated. They don't always hit the 5-minute target, but they've made great strides.

- Contractor–customer relationships. A building construction company found that most of their customer dissatisfaction was found in misunderstandings regarding customer-requested changes to the building once the plans were finalized. The contractors started to measure the number of change orders. After analyzing the data, they found that by using better listening skills upfront and using a checklist the customer could sign off to show acknowledgment of the plan, they were able to reduce change orders due to better communication and understanding from the customer's perspective.

- Bank employee–customer relationships. Most banks crave to be the one stop for all your financial needs. They want to build stronger relationships with their customers and gain more "share of wallet." One bank decided that if they were going to forge strong customer relationships it would help if employees remembered customer names. They began measuring the number of times that employees greeted a customer by name. Every time they greeted a customer by name, each employee made a tick mark on a piece of paper. The tick marks were added up at the end of the day, compiled at the end of the week, and posted in the employee break area. Employees managed the process themselves. They began to concentrate on remembering names. They shared different memory tricks with each other. They were successful, had some fun, and customers got personalized service—which was the goal. Sound trivial? How do you feel when you walk into a business where they know your name? Don't you feel like there's a relationship there? Simple things sometimes work the best.

We know that there are skeptics who think, "What if an employee fudges his numbers?" Unlike the call center cited earlier in the chapter, there were no penalties associated with this measurement. It was done in the spirit of improvement. Also, the employees came up with the idea and managed the process themselves—the bank manager didn't mandate it. Fudging the numbers served no purpose.

- Everything Speaks Checklist results. Another company was committed to improving the physical environment of the organization. Using the Everything Speaks Checklists, they measured the weekly total of unsatisfactory ratings. The objective, of course, was to get that number to zero. They didn't always hit the goal, but attention to detail improved.

- Internal relationships. Internal computer help desks are often targets of employee wrath. One help desk determined that a key measure of success was help tickets closed on one contact. They started tracking help tickets that required more than one contact. Once they had the data, they were able to develop solutions to the multiple contact problems.

Of course, these are just examples. Each one of them, however, was connected to the bigger picture of service improvement. In each case, the workgroup determined what to measure and was able to impact the results. The approach was a win for everyone.

Posting Customer Satisfaction and Local Measurements

If employees don't know the results of service measurements, they can't be expected to take action to improve the results. Not communicating measurement results is like having a gas gauge that works but putting it in the trunk of the car. The measurement is there, but the information is pretty useless. Service measurements should be highly visible to employees, easy to interpret, and up to date.

A lot of leaders are afraid to share measurement results— particularly formal, customer satisfaction data. They are afraid that the information might "leak out" and hurt the organization. So these leaders keep the data to themselves and share them on a *need-to-know* basis. The problem with that approach is that the frontline employees are usually the ones who can directly improve service. They are the ones that *need to know*. Take the risk and share the information.

We visited a hospital that was truly committed to communicating customer satisfaction information with their employees. This hospital used Press Ganey (discussed earlier) for their formal measurement process. They posted the scores in public areas throughout the hospital. We asked if this was a wise thing to do— after all, patients could see the scores. The leader's answer was inspiring: "If we say we're going to be the best, then we're going to put up or shut up. Putting the scores in public areas shows how much we believe in this stuff."

And the employees responded. We saw countless employees checking out the scores that were just posted to see how they were doing. And, even though they were doing well, they were determined to get better.

Measurement Charts

One of the initial functions of the Service Improvement Team as it pertains to measurement is to develop a "branded" measurement chart format that all areas of the organization can use for their local measurements. By "branded" we mean that the format of the charts is standardized. This allows anyone walking through any area to identify that area's service improvement measurement charts. The information tracked will obviously vary by area, but the overall look of the charts will be the same.

There are many styles of measurement charts; the main thing is to keep it simple. Its purpose is to provide a quick visual regarding service progress. Figure 8.5 is an example of a simple measurement chart that is flexible enough to use in most circumstances. In this case it's used to chart average wait times in a physician's office.

The chart is roughly poster-size and is easy to read. The vertical axis can be adapted to represent a variety of measurements such as wait times, questions answered, towels delivered, service requests fulfilled, and so on. It's up to the workgroup to determine what's measured. The horizontal axis usually denotes units of time. Measurements (average wait times in Figure 8.5) are posted each week and tracked. The information gleaned from the charts becomes the foundation for service improvement discussions.

We recommend standardized measurement charts so that they can be branded to your company's service improvement effort. Any time an employee sees one of these charts they should

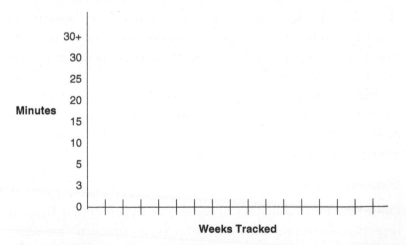

Figure 8.5 Process: Waiting Room Time (Go to www.Unleashing-Excellence.com to download a customizable copy of this form.)

immediately know a service factor is being measured. An executive can visit any area and immediately seek out measurement data without having to rummage through a bunch of forms.

Where to Post the Measurement Charts

What do Olympic runners do as soon as they finish a race? They look at the clock to see how they did. Gymnasts look at the score they received. You can feel the excitement in the air as they wait for the score. Measurement charts must be prominently posted to have an impact on employees. We've already talked about the hospital that publicly displayed their measurements, but you may not be comfortable going to that extreme—yet. But *employees* should be able to see the charts as often as possible. Break rooms, office bulletin boards, and other "backstage" areas are all appropriate as long as employees *can't miss them*. Having the charts displayed not only keeps employees updated on results, it also reminds employees to give great service. Take a walk through your employee areas tomorrow. What tells them how they are doing?

Keeping Measurement Charts Updated

Few things scream "flavor-of-the-month program" louder than outdated measurement displays. One call center employee told us that his department had a huge chart on the wall with customer satisfaction scores. The figures were 8 months out of date. This causes two problems:

1. It's hard for employees to take the service measurements seriously if the organization doesn't.
2. It's hard to act on old information. How does an employee know if a new process or behavior has an impact if he doesn't get feedback for 8 months?

Every employee can help keep the charts up to date. You can rotate the responsibility or the charts can be updated during weekly team meetings. Participation is the key. The Service

Improvement Team member responsible for the Measurement Leadership Action, along with his or her subteam, should coordinate communication, distribution, and education regarding the measurement process. Thereafter, the individual workgroups are responsible for keeping the charts up to date.

How Many Measurements

At some point, we've all suffered through this scenario: You attend a business update. One speaker after another stands at the front of the room explaining their business metrics. Each goes through about 30 information-jammed PowerPoint slides, introducing each one with, "I know you can't read this." They make an attempt to use a laser pointer to highlight important points, but it's too late. Your mind has already gone numb from overload.

Most organizations measure hundreds, even thousands, of performance factors. Each one may be important to the organization's ongoing success. For local measurements branded to the service improvement effort, however, focus on two to three measurements at the most. You should also post key elements of overall customer satisfaction survey data, but two to three local measurements is a small enough number to keep employees engaged in tracking the measurements. The exact number will depend on your operation and the complexity of the service factors being tackled. Just don't overwhelm the team.

Setting Goals

Goal setting is not always appropriate for the measurement process. For the Housekeeping example cited earlier, the objective was to track delays in completing room assignments. Once the true culprit of delays was determined, the team went on to other measurements. In other cases goal setting is appropriate. The physician's office cited earlier set a goal of seeing patients within a 5-minute window of the appointment time. The measurement chart, therefore, should reflect performance in relation to the goal. It might look like the chart in Figure 8.6. All

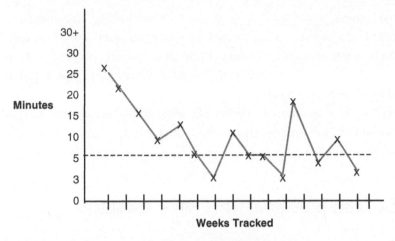

Figure 8.6   Process: Waiting Room Wait Time

employees can easily see how the actual wait time compares to the goal. By looking at the chart, the team can discuss what's having the greatest impact on wait times. They can see the occasional spikes where the wait time increased above the goal. What happened that week? The measurement and goal provide the foundation for what should be a lively discussion.

When to Change Measurements

As noted earlier in the chapter, each workgroup should identify two to three service measurements that apply to their operation. When should the workgroup stop measuring a particular factor and choose another measurement? It depends upon the situation, of course, but the team should collaboratively decide to move on to other issues if:

1. The issue has been solved (i.e., the Housekeeper room-readiness issue).
2. The team is consistently achieving targeted goals (i.e., the physician's office wait time).

One purpose of service measurement is to engage all employees in the process. If measurements become stale or lose their usefulness, employees lose interest. Concluding the measurement of a service element and selecting another is a great time for a celebration. Celebration highlights the success of the effort and gathers energy around the new measurement. The decision should be a team effort. The team should also agree to be wary of backsliding in any of the service elements that are no longer measured. Revisit past measurement charts to ensure continued service excellence.

The Service Improvement Team's Role in Measurement

Noting that some of these have already been mentioned, the Service Improvement Team has several roles and responsibilities in regard to making the Measurement Leadership Action a success. It first must establish some guiding principles. These might include:

- Focus measurement on process improvement, not on blaming individuals.
- Link measures to the Service Philosophy or Service Standards.
- Involve all employees in the process.
- Measure and track no more than three local measures at a time.
- Avoid negative impact on one process as a consequence of improving another process.
- Post branded measurement charts in areas where employees can see the results.
- Tie goal setting and measurement together.
- Seek input from employees on how to reach goals.
- Give recognition for meeting goals, then choose another measurement.

The Measurement subteam should assist workgroups in determining what to measure, especially those workgroups who are having difficulty getting started. The subteam will develop the branded measurement charts as well as the procedures for workgroups to use in determining what to measure and how to use the results as a tool for improvement. It will also be their role to monitor the charts to ensure all departments are participating and charts are kept up to date.

The Leader's Role in Measurement

If the workgroup's leader doesn't take the measurement process seriously, it's doubtful that the workgroup will take it seriously. The leader plays an important role in the measurement process. He or she certainly shouldn't dictate what's measured, but he or she must ensure that service measurements play a prominent role in the operation.

The main thing is to build an atmosphere of "no bad news" with local measurements. Remember the scenario at the call center? Because employees were penalized based on the measurement, they just worked around the system. Use the measurements as a tool for discussion and improvement, not penalties. Figure 8.7 provides guidelines for leaders in service measurement.

Concluding Thoughts

Be prepared for some confusion when beginning the service measurement process. Sometimes the workgroup will struggle with identifying things to measure. If necessary, get the Service Improvement Team measurement subteam to assist. Use the Service Standards and Service Maps to help the team identify areas of measurement opportunity. Once the measurement process is under way, as long as it is well managed, most organizations are delighted with the results. They find that performance improves simply because attention is focused on the service factor being

- Collaborate with the Service Improvement Team in obtaining measurement charts and understanding how to use the charts. The Service Improvement Team can provide ideas and guidelines on the measurement process.
- Meet with the workgroup to identify service elements for measurement. Department Service Maps can provide direction on appropriate measures.
- Ensure that measurement charts are prominently posted in employee areas.
- Ensure that measurement charts are kept up to date. Updating the charts should be a collaborative effort, but the leader must ensure that it's done.
- Refer to the measurement information often and use the information as a foundation for discussion and problem solving. Ask questions about the information.
- Ensure a "no bad news" environment regarding the service measurement data. If the data is used to penalize the workgroup, employees will disengage from the process. Use the information to focus on service improvement.
- Celebrate achievement of a goal or success in identifying or solving a service problem.
- Revisit past measurement charts to ensure no backsliding has occurred.

Figure 8.7   Guidelines for Leaders in Local Measurements

measured. These same organizations find solutions to service problems that have been haunting them for years. Effective measurements serve as a scorecard on the journey to service excellence.

Service Improvement Team Action Steps

- Create baseline measurements using key business metrics.
- Develop a customer satisfaction survey instrument or engage a vendor to implement a survey.
- Develop measurement chart formats and procedures.

- Communicate possible service improvement measurements and educate everyone on the importance of measurement and the measurement procedures.
- Let the workgroups choose what to measure.
- Ensure that every area workgroup is measuring service.
- Display the measurement charts in visible areas for employees to see.
- Have continual reminders that the focus of measurement is on the process, not on blaming people.
- Ask the workgroup to identify actions for improving scores.
- Let the workgroup set its own goals.
- Use measurement as a foundation for discussion and problem solving.

Pitfalls to Avoid

- Don't dictate local measurements.
- Don't ignore the charts.
- Don't post measurement charts where customers can see them.
- Don't punish the workgroup for not meeting goals. Find out why they are not meeting the goals and determine how you can help.
- Don't let the measurements go unchanged once they have achieved optimum levels.
- Don't let achievements or efforts go unrecognized or uncelebrated.

Chapter Nine

RECOGNITION

"I was cashing a check at the bank. It wasn't crowded, but I had to wait for one of the tellers to finish up something else before she helped me. As she started counting my money back to me, I noticed an 'employee of the month' ribbon on her nametag. This 'employee of the month' must've been having an off day, because she definitely wasn't doing anything to make me feel special. Anyway, I asked her what she did to win the award. She said, 'I don't know, I guess it was my turn.' She never even made eye contact."

This scenario misses the whole point of recognition, doesn't it? Unfortunately, the "just my turn" syndrome is alive and well in the recognition programs of many organizations. In these organizations recognition has become a joke and a chore.

This chapter will focus on making recognition an effective part of your service improvement process. Some of the ideas might seem more suited to large organizations, but they're just as effective in small companies. It's only the scale that's different.

The Emotional Connection

You know how you feel when you do something nice for some-one? It could be something unexpected for a spouse, a friend, or even someone you don't know. It's just a good deed. It feels pretty good to help someone. You don't always expect recognition for your actions, but deep down, you do appreciate it when someone notices what you did.

The word *recognition* actually comes from a Latin word mean-ing "to know again." Effective recognition should help an employee *know again* the feeling he or she experienced when providing excellent service. When someone acknowledges our performance we *know again* the good feelings we experienced when doing the good deed. That emotional connection is the key to successful recognition.

Keep this emotional connection in mind as we discuss various types of recognition. The more that recognition stirs the emo-tions of your employees, the more powerful it will be. Remember the bank teller at the beginning of the chapter? She didn't even know why she was employee of the month! How much pride could there be in that situation? Contrast that example with one that occurred in another organization: An employee was to be sur-prised with an award for excellent performance. Her manager arranged for the award to be given at the end of the day so that the employee's husband and daughter could attend the ceremony. The ceremony was nothing elaborate or expensive, but imagine the emotional impact of being recognized for her performance with her family present. Being a hero in front of your family is about the ultimate in pride. You can't put a price tag on that.

Consulting colleague Dee Hansford shared the following story with us:

> "While managing the Cast Recognition function at Disney, I relied on one of our exceptional photographers to take cast member portraits as part of an award ceremony. On the day of the event, our photographer arrived and went about the job in his usual excellent manner, making each cast member

feel special. I knew him well, however, and could tell that something was bothering him. On a break I asked him about it. He confessed that his mother had passed away the night before after a long illness, but rather than let me or our cast members down, he decided to come and work the event.

"Now, I ask you, how do you recognize such dedication and commitment? After much thought and discussion, we made reservations for him and his family at Disney's Hoop-De-Doo Revue at Fort Wilderness. He called later to tell me that it was the first time his family wasn't under incredible stress and the first time he had heard his young son laugh in many, many months. He told me he would never forget the kindness shown to his family during that very trying time. I learned the lasting power of recognition that day."

Dee's story has nothing to do with buying tickets for a show. It has everything to do with the thought that went into how to best recognize someone who did a stellar job while under stressful family conditions. Giving him and his family a brief respite from the stress is a great example of personalized recognition.

A wonderful recognition tool for making an emotional connection is storytelling. When you recognize an employee's performance, use storytelling to describe what he or she did to receive the recognition. Bring the experience to life. Let the employee and those present *know again* what happened and the impact it had on the customer. Better yet, if appropriate, let the employee (and/or coworkers) join in the storytelling. This takes some forethought, but it's worth every minute of planning.

Types of Recognition

This chapter will focus on three types of recognition:

- manager-to-employee
- peer-to-peer
- company-to-employee

We'll look at each one and discuss ideas for making them powerful. Keep the emotional connection in mind as you develop ideas for your organization's recognition efforts.

Manager-to-Employee Recognition

This is the most powerful form of recognition. The most influential person in our work lives is usually our immediate supervisor. Even if we don't like our supervisor, we still want him or her to appreciate the work we do. As a matter of fact, research on employee turnover shows that lack of recognition from the immediate boss is a top reason for employee defection. Just about everyone has had a boss who only comments on the negative. Isn't it hard to give your all when you only hear about problems from your boss? On the other hand, when your supervisor comments positively on something you've done, even if it's just a brief comment, you have at least a moment in which all is right with the world. Everyone appreciates being appreciated.

A key to the success of manager-to-employee recognition is *immediacy*. The closer the recognition comes to the actual behavior, the greater the likelihood that the employee will be motivated to repeat the behavior. Let's use a hospital as an example. An obviously anxious person comes in to the hospital and is clearly lost. A custodian approaches her and asks if he can assist. The customer, tears in her eyes, asks for directions to the Intensive Care Unit. The custodian escorts her to the proper elevator and gets her headed to the right floor, ensuring that she knows her way. The custodian's demeanor shows that he cares. This employee *knows* that he has done something special. His emotions are elevated because he knows. If his supervisor sees or hears about this action, the most powerful thing she can do is immediately recognize the performance. The immediacy of the praise dramatically increases the likelihood that the custodian will repeat the behavior in the future. Sounds somewhat manipulative, doesn't it? It's not. It's good human relations and it's good business. The same principle applies in your organization, no matter the size.

The challenge for most of us as leaders is that we're so busy we don't take the time to notice the good things happening around us. It's not that we don't *want* to thank employees—we just don't always remember to do it. It's like remembering to get the oil changed in your car. We know that we should get it changed every 3,000 to 5,000 miles, but it's hard to remember to do it. But if you don't, you're headed for trouble down the road—just like failing to recognize employees for good work. Many auto repair shops now place a sticker on the car windshield to remind us when it's time for an oil change. They've given us a tool to follow through on our good intentions. We recommend developing a tool to remind leaders to "catch people doing things right." Figure 9.1 is an example of such a tool. It's simply a card, small enough to fit in a pocket, wallet, purse, or organizer, and can be given to any employee caught providing excellent service.

There's space on the card to write the employee's name and what he or she did to receive recognition. The card is given to the employee *on the spot.* Any member of management can give any employee a recognition card (we'll discuss peer-to-peer recognition in the next section).

Some organizations have a drop box in which the recognized employee can submit the card for a month-end drawing. Do that if you want to, but remember that the real power is the immediate

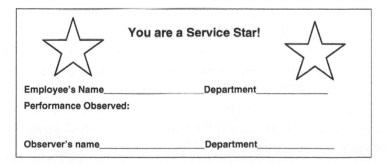

Figure 9.1 On-the-Spot Recognition Card (Go to www.UnleashingEx-cellence.com to download a customizable copy of this form.)

recognition. The purpose of the card is to remind management that they are supposed to be looking for examples of excellent service and providing recognition. It's not about the *card*; it's about the *emotion*.

One client wanted to do everything they could to encourage the leadership team to recognize employees who delivered excellent service. They developed a toolkit, even purchased cardboard toolboxes branded to their service initiative, and filled it with recognition cards, discount coupons, buttons, and a copy of the book *1001 Ways to Recognize Employees*, by Bob Nelson. Leaders appreciated the effort and, more importantly, used the tools to acknowledge strong performance.

Public recognition is powerful. Other employees get to share in the celebration. It doesn't have to take place in an assembly; it's public recognition even if only one or two other employees are there. Some managers push back on this idea by insisting, "Some of my employees *hate* to be recognized in public. They find it embarrassing." Fine. Since the manager clearly knows who these employees are, we simply advise them to recognize those employees in private. Life just doesn't have to be that hard.

Peer-to-Peer Recognition

"Our department was going through a tough time. We were really understaffed and I knew we were close to causing some major screw-ups for customers. Kaye was the manager of another department that we worked with frequently. She personally pitched in and helped us out, adding to her own heavy workload. We got through in good shape— thanks to Kaye. We had a plaque made for her with gloves in an applause pose and a note that said how much we appreciated her. Kaye told us many times that the plaque was the most meaningful recognition of her career."

Yes, the plaque cost a few dollars, but the effect was priceless. Peer-to-peer recognition is powerful.

Most likely, when an employee is observed providing excellent customer service, it is a peer who observes it. Doesn't it make sense to encourage peers to recognize each other? Peer-to-peer recognition builds a sense of teamwork and family.

As mentioned in Chapter 5, First Financial Bankshares sends out a Wow! e-mail blast for any employee who has been recognized by a peer for going above and beyond in customer service. The Wow! e-mail identifies the employee, their job position, and what they did to deliver exemplary service. This approach not only recognizes employees, it keeps a continuous focus on service excellence.

Another banking client, Machias Savings Bank of Machias, Maine, was so interested in building peer-to-peer recognition that the bank gave each department a budget to be used for recognizing other areas of the bank that provided excellent internal service. One department, for example, used their budget to recognize another department by bringing in a masseuse to provide a day of chair massages (now that's recognition!). By providing the resources to encourage peer-to-peer recognition, the bank reinforced their seriousness and commitment to service improvement.

Go back to the earlier chapters on Communication and Training. As you roll out the service initiative and provide ongoing communication, make sure you stress peer-to-peer recognition. During the training sessions, highlight the importance of catching each other giving great service. Not everyone will do it, but many will with a little encouragement. Again, a tool is useful here. Why not provide your employees with the same recognition cards shown in Figure 9.1? Some organizations have designed a special card for peer-to-peer recognition so that they can recognize each other not only for customer service, but for just about *any* outstanding behavior. Examples include:

- teamwork
- covering a shift so an employee can get to a son/daughter event
- helping a coworker through a tough time
- solving a departmental problem

One of the reasons that this approach is powerful is that it increases the likelihood that those employees who work in support areas will be recognized for service. Usually the glory goes to customer-facing employees. We know that support areas are critical to customer service success, but we don't always treat them that way. Recognition should flow throughout the organization. Figure 9.2 is an example of a cross departmental recognition tool you can customize to your operation.

Before moving on to company-to-employee recognition, a point needs to be made about documentation: Any form of recognition—manager-to-employee, peer-to-peer, or company-to-employee—should be documented on the employee's record card or file. Service excellence recognition should play an important role in performance appraisals, pay increases, promotions, and job transfers, so documentation is critical. It's pretty embarrassing to give a person a "needs development" for a service factor on a performance appraisal, only to be handed a stack of service recognition cards he's earned during the year.

Thanks for Your Help!

Employee's Name _____ Department _____
Comments:

My Name _____ My Department _____

Your Performance Strengthens the Whole Team!

Figure 9.2 Cross-Departmental Recognition Card (Go to www.UnleashingExcellence.com to download a customizable copy of this form.)

Make sure recognition is documented. The employee has earned it.

Company-to-Employee Recognition

Most organizations already have some kind of formal company-to-employee recognition program. Employee of the Month and Employee of the Year programs abound, and we fully support them. The problem, however, is that this is the only type of recognition a lot of companies use. There are only two possible outcomes when that's the case:

1. After a while, the same people receive the award over and over because they are the ones who deserve it. Everyone else is left out.
2. People who don't deserve the award get it because everyone else has gotten it: the "it's my turn" syndrome.

By using all of the recognition techniques in this chapter, *all* employees have the opportunity to be recognized. Just about everyone does *something* good at some point. If not, should that employee even be working in your company?

That being said, we do feel it's important to acknowledge your stellar performers with company-to-employee recognition. The top employees should be recognized as the best of the best service providers. They deserve it. You don't want to lose these employees! Remember, one of the top reasons that employees defect is because they feel taken for granted. Many times the only recognition excellent performers get is an increased workload. Your best performers need to know that you know they are your best performers.

Seminole Community College (SCC), located in Central Florida, knows that the 10 days of school registration that precede every semester have a tremendous effect on the image of the college within the student body and the Central Florida community itself.

The experience can also be a very emotional time for the young student, middle-age student, or older student who is looking to change their life through education and the opportunities it can bring. The Service Improvement Team created what they called the "10 Days of Service Excellence" recognition program to call attention to the importance each staff member has on the student experience during this period.

Here's how their recognition program works: Immediately after registering for classes, students are asked a series of seven questions that tie into the school's Service Standards. For example, one of their Service Standards is "Competent" and the question asked on the survey is: "How would you rate the SCC staff member who helped you today for demonstrating an ability to help you—or directing you to someone who could help?" To keep it in the context of a school environment, the survey asks the students to respond to the questions by giving a grade of A through F. In addition, each staff member involved in the registration process, upon completion of their interaction with a student, is asked to give the student a card titled "Tell It Like It Is" with the staff member's name written on it. The card asks the student to go to the nearby computer kiosk and complete a web-based 24/7 survey. At the end of the day, the surveys are compiled and tallied. The staff member receiving the highest number of positive ratings for service excellence for that day is the winner. On the following day, Dr. James Henningsen, the Vice President for Student Success and Chairperson of the Service Improvement Team, personally goes to the college campus of the winner and, in front of their peers, congratulates them, presents them with a Target gift card, and has a photo taken for the college newsletter. At the next Board of Trustees meeting, all of the winners are introduced, praised, and recognized for their commitment to serving students and changing lives (which is the essence of the college's Service Philosophy).

Because the surveys are conducted through a variety of means, including on-the-spot interviews and computer self-administered surveys, SCC believes they are recognizing top performers and collecting valuable student feedback that will help improve their service. Dr. Henningsen says, "We want to make our staff feel special, let them know they are appreciated, and also set them up to be role models for other staff members, thus encouraging others to help change student lives." The program has been a huge success and has resulted in significant improvements in the college's satisfaction metrics across all areas. In fact, the service satisfaction rates were the highest during the 10 Days of Service Excellence than at any time throughout the registration window.

Figure 9.3 provides a flowchart for a formal recognition process. It ensures that deserving employees receive the top, formal recognition. The process should be taken seriously and should be well publicized. The award ceremony should be something very special that truly acknowledges the accomplishment and creates a lasting memory. Some organizations provide a significant memento of the accomplishment for which the employee is being recognized. One company rewards the winners of their formal recognition program with a porcelain ballerina. This exquisite statuette has been established as the symbol of a dedicated individual who plans, practices, and rehearses to always

1. Nomination form completed by co-workers(s).
2. Form dropped in collection box or sent to appropriate representative.
3. Nominee's name logged.
4. Nominee's name sent to recognition committee.
5. Recognition committee validates criteria with assistance from department leader, co-workers, customers.
6. If criteria are met, nominee's name continues in process. If criteria are not met, name is withdrawn, but employee receives note of congratulations for nomination.
7. Recognition committee conducts final processing and selects recipients.
8. Recipients notified of celebration date and time.
9. Celebration!

Figure 9.3   Formal Recognition Process Flow

ensure a flawless performance the first time. The statuette is proudly displayed by the select few who earn it.

The Question of Monetary Rewards

Giving monetary rewards for service excellence is a touchy subject. Some organizations believe in monetary rewards wholeheartedly, and, if this works for your company, stick with it. Few people would turn down money. If you are in the process of crafting a recognition program, however, and haven't made a decision on monetary awards, we highly suggest you avoid giving money for giving great service. The whole objective of the service improvement process is to make service excellence part of the culture. If employees only give great service if they get paid extra for it, service excellence is not inculturated. Periodic drawings for those who receive recognition cards (discussed earlier) can be okay as long as the drawings don't become the point. The emotion of the recognition is the point. Many will disagree with us on the money issue, but we've seen monetary recognition programs degenerate into "I'll only do it if you pay me" situations. And once you start such a monetary reward program, it quickly becomes an entitlement, making it very difficult to ever eliminate.

Concluding Thoughts

Many leaders underestimate the value of service recognition. Employees themselves sometimes disregard its importance. In fact, a study was done in which employees representing several industries were asked if they needed encouragement to perform at their best. Almost all of the employees said no, they didn't need encouragement. Further study, however, revealed that the researchers worded the question incorrectly. The respondents were saying that they didn't *need* encouragement to perform at their best. None of us likes to admit that we need outside reinforcement to do a good job. When asked the question a different way ("When you get recognition from your boss, does it help you to perform at your best?"), 98 percent of the respondents said yes. In other words, we are willing to admit that recognition *helps* us perform better.

The keys to an effective recognition program are to ensure that the correct behaviors are recognized, the timing of the recognition is as close to the actual behavior as possible, and that the recognition contains an emotional component. A well-planned recognition program can serve as a compass for the service improvement effort. Catching employees doing things right lets them know that they are headed in the right direction.

Service Improvement Team Action Steps

- Ensure that recognition is strategically linked to the overall service improvement effort.
- Review current recognition practices to determine if they are consistent with the Service Standards as well as with other elements of the initiative.
- Create recognition tools that cover the three key areas of recognition—manager-to-employee, peer-to-peer, and company-to-employee.
- Communicate and train all management and frontline employees on the importance of recognizing service excellence.
- Provide ongoing emphasis on the emotional component of recognition.

Pitfalls to Avoid

- Don't allow the "it's just my turn" syndrome to creep into the organization's recognition efforts.

- Don't allow monetary rewards or prizes to distill the emotional element of recognition.
- Don't forget to document all recognition in the employee's file or record card.
- Don't allow time to pass before recognizing excellent behavior. Immediacy is vital.

Chapter Ten

SERVICE OBSTACLE SYSTEM

"A neighbor was having some work done on his property and the workers accidentally cut the buried phone lines leading to *my* house. We have a line for our private phone as well as several lines for our in-home business. All were cut. Using my cell phone, I called the phone company and went through the standard, irritating phone tree of 'press 1 for this' and 'press 2 for that.' Once I made my selection I waited on hold for 20 minutes, all the while hearing a recorded voice saying how important my call was. Right.

"When a representative finally picked up, I found him to be very personable. After I explained the problem, he told me they could have a technician out the next day to repair the residential line. 'But what about my business lines?' I asked. There was a long pause before he answered, and his voice had lost some of its brightness. 'You'll have to talk to the small business department for that.' I knew that would mean going through the same hassle of getting to a live person, so I said, 'Wait a minute, do the same technicians handle the residential and business line repairs?' He quietly replied that they do. 'Then why can't YOU just schedule the whole thing?' And in a voice that betrayed his embarrassment he replied, 'Because that's not the way our system works.'"

How many times have you been so frustrated by a company's processes that it didn't matter how friendly the employees were? The employee in the previous story was set up to fail, and he knew it. When employees are set up to fail, you can see it in their faces and you can hear it in their voices. When employees know they can't win, they disengage from the customer experience and progressively bury their emotions. It's only natural that they disengage. Most of us have a strong fear of humiliation. If you've ever been humiliated (and who hasn't?) you know how it feels. Panic sets in and your mind races to save face. Humiliation is emotionally draining and most of us can't handle much of it—we'll do almost anything to avoid it.

If the system sets an employee up to fail and to be humiliated, a natural reaction is for him to shut off his emotions and protect his dignity. Why doesn't the employee seem to care? Because he once did care and got blamed even though there was nothing he could do to help you. The only way he could protect his dignity was to stop caring. Everyone loses when that happens.

In this chapter we'll look at ways to continually improve the level of service that your organization provides. We'll focus heavily on setting employees up for success and arming them with the tools that make them service heroes.

Service Heroes

When your organization sets you up to be a hero, you *want* to help customers. It's rewarding to help customers when you know you're supported—you're going to be a hero. Helping re-unite lost children and parents at Disney World is a great example of this principle in action. If you've ever lost sight of your child in a crowd, you know the terror that overwhelms you. Just imagine how many parents and children this happens to in a crowded place like Disney World. So they've put a system in place. Let's say that a cast member sees a parent frantically looking for his lost child. Somewhere else another cast member sees a crying child looking for her parents. There is a single phone number for both cast members to call (it's called Lost Parents), and parent and child can be re-united immediately. The family is so excited to be re-united that they treat those two employees as heroes. The parents are thrilled, the child is happy, and the employees are heroes. Everybody wins. That's the power of setting employees up for success.

Removing Service Obstacles

One of the most important jobs of a leader in a service improvement initiative is to help remove obstacles that keep employees from giving great service. Unfortunately, employees usually think of their leaders as people who *put* obstacles in front of them:

- "From now on, a manager must approve all returns over $200."
- "There will be a $25 per incident charge for a customer to speak to a technician about a computer problem."
- "You cannot give a customer an empty cup for water. We are now using cup stock to track drink sales. If a customer really wants an empty cup, you have to charge them 50 cents."

We're sure that you can add to this list of infuriating rules. On the other hand, a service-oriented organization searches for ways to make the customer experience easier and more pleasant. They look at their processes and ask, "How can we make this better?" When processes are more customer friendly, employees are more customer friendly.

The Teaching Company brings America's best professors into your home or car by providing audio lectures. They offer over 250 courses for life-long learners without the stress of homework or exams. Their customer service is impeccable due in part to the design of their processes. They've streamlined the purchase process so that courses are ideally suited to the tastes, demands, and interests of the customer. The Teaching Company keeps detailed data on every customer's purchases and they continually survey the customer's interests and solicit feedback on previous purchases. As a valued customer, they provide you with significant discounts, participation in the selection of new courses and professors, and free lectures and updates on areas of interest. These processes allow employees to engage with the customer on a personalized basis to ensure every course taken is extremely rewarding. All obstacles that would prevent an employee from delivering excellent service have been removed from the system. Customers are happy and employees are happy.

Removing obstacles doesn't have to be complicated. In fact, it's usually just a matter of stepping back and asking what the *real* problem is. Buying a computer provides a good example. Buying a new home computer is exciting for most people. Setting up a new home computer is maddening for most people. All of the equipment, cords, disks, and manuals are overwhelming. Because most of us have been in the situation, it's easy to picture the poor customer sitting on the floor, surrounded by all of that equipment, frustrated out of his mind. Computer company help desks are bombarded by calls from frustrated customers trying to assemble these demon machines. As more people bought computers, more people needed help from help desks. The solution to increased call volume was to add more employees, add automated phone trees, and offer online help (as if you could get online with the computer in pieces around you). And customers got madder and madder. Finally, some smart person asked, "What's *really* the problem here?" The problem was that the computer was too hard to assemble! So what can be done to solve that problem? One solution has been to provide a one-page "quick setup" guide with the computer and to color code the cables with the proper inputs in the computer. The customer just matches up the colors. It's not foolproof, and most computer hardware and software companies have a long way to go to be customer friendly, but the setup process is a lot easier than it used to be.

Identifying Service Obstacles

Your employees are your best source for identifying and solving service problems. Customers are also a great source of information, but employees see the ongoing, recurring problems. They're also the ones who bear the wrath of customers' frustrations, so they have a vested interest in ongoing process improvement.

Figure 10.1 is a Continuous Service Improvement meeting agenda. The objective is to bring together your employees on a regular basis to talk about barriers to delivering great service. It's an open discussion in which anyone can bring up problems that need a solution. The group then decides what problems to actually tackle. The workgroup owns the process.

Of course, real life is never as clean and easy as the agenda in Figure 10.1. There will be disagreements and frustrations as service issues are discussed. But the more faithful you are about holding these service improvement meetings and really doing something about the key problems, the more your employees will trust the process and tolerate its imperfections.

Our recommendation is that every department conduct a Continuous Service Improvement meeting at least once a quarter, preferably once a month. Imagine the power of having every department identify and solve 12 customer service obstacles every year. Your company will leave less dedicated organizations in the dust.

If you run a small organization or are responsible for a single department, you can invite all employees to the monthly meetings. You might not get 100 percent attendance, but at least everyone has the chance to participate. A large company implementing a service improvement effort will probably hold departmental meetings for all areas of the company. The important thing is that every area of the company is seeking ways to eliminate service barriers.

1. Put employees at ease by holding the meeting in a distraction-free environment. Silence pagers, phones, etc.

2. State the purpose of the discussion: To identify obstacles that are in the way of delivering exceptional customer service to our external and internal customers.

3. Re-emphasize that continuous improvement is not directed at blaming people, but at improving processes.

4. Establish a cooperative environment at the meeting, following the rules for successful brainstorming:
   - Title flipchart: What keeps me from delivering exceptional service?
   - Set allotted time for brainstorming.
   - Record all obstacles on flipchart.
   - Encourage all participation, not permitting critical comments.

5. After discussion, select one or two obstacles that are a major source of customer complaints and frustration.

6. Generate as many potential solutions to the obstacle as possible. Often, the solution will be generated on the spot. The key is to keep an open mind and build on ideas. While not every solution presented will be feasible, it's important to respect the contribution.

7. For those solutions that will require time and study to implement, discuss and agree on who will be responsible to work on a solution and others who need to be involved. The more involvement from the team, the greater the resulting buy-in.

8. Set a date to report back on status of obstacle and solution.

9. Thank employees for being honest in the session and express confidence in their ability to come up with solutions and your willingness to help them.

Figure 10.1 Continuous Service Improvement Meeting Agenda (Go to www.UnleashingExcellence.com to download a customizable copy of this form.)

The Role of the Service Improvement Team

If one area of the company is suffering with a service problem, it's likely that another area has a similar issue. We were conducting a seminar for a client and were helping them to identify service problems and brainstorm solutions. One manager described the way his department had triumphed over a long-term problem. Another seminar participant jumped from her chair and yelled, "I need to talk to you! What's your phone number?" The two of them jokingly exaggerated a ceremony of exchanging business cards, and everyone laughed at the dramatization. What's important, however, is that one department's problem was solved by another department's solution.

Imagine if that kind of communication was the norm in your business. Your company could become one of those legendary "learning organizations" we hear so much about. In small companies, this kind of sharing can happen in meetings or just from leadership keeping alert to problems and solutions. It doesn't have to be complicated; it just has to be deliberate.

Larger organizations will need to systematize the communication process. The champion and subteam of the Service Obstacle System Leadership Action are responsible for ensuring not only that all areas of the organization are addressing obstacles, but also that solutions are leveraged around the organization. The subteam should receive the meeting minutes from the departments and, in their subteam meetings, discuss what is happening and determine how to best leverage successes. When employees see action being taken, buy-in increases as does the credibility of the entire service initiative.

LYNX, a bus transit company in Orlando, Florida, wanted to begin this kind of communication from day one of their service excellence training classes. They wanted to show the benefits of everyone being involved in identifying and solving service issues. After the introductions of why the service improvement process was being initiated in the organization, the trainer would pass around a sheet asking participants to write down any items they felt were preventing them from delivering excellent service. They were also asked to identify possible solutions to the problems. At the end of each class, the obstacle sheets were collected and the obstacles recorded. As their Service Obstacle System subteam was still in the process of being formed, the director of training took on their initial duties. She contacted the appropriate department for addressing a particular obstacle and would follow-up until a resolution was reached. A report with the obstacles and close-out dates was distributed to every new service excellence training class so they could see what had already been brought up, what was being worked on, and what had been closed out. Seventy-six action items were closed during the first year.

A Formal Service Obstacle System

You've probably noticed that one of the premises of this chapter (as well as this book) is that most customer service problems can and should be solved by the people who are closest to the situation. Typically, those people are your frontline employees. The processes and systems we've discussed, for the most part, are designed to assist the frontline in providing excellent service. You may be wondering, however, about the larger, organization-wide service issues that truly require an organization-wide solution. The computer help line situation discussed earlier is a good example. In a large technology company, the help line employees can't change the way the computers are built. But they *can* communicate the problems customers have trying to assemble the computers. The Service Obstacle System is a formal problem resolution process designed to handle such issues in large companies.

Designing a Formal Service Obstacle System

The Service Improvement Team member who is responsible for this Leadership Action will need to pull together a subteam of talented individuals who have expertise and knowledge in several different areas. This might consist of someone from IT, customer service, operations, administration, and someone with overall knowledge of how the entire organization's flow of communication works. The purpose of this subteam will be to design the format and flow of the system, educate everyone on how to use the system, and monitor its use.

More than likely, it will need to be an automated system, although many organizations prefer to use a paper-based system. Regardless of the approach you choose, your formal Service Obstacle System should do the following:

- Provide a mechanism for employees to identify an obstacle to service excellence.
- Clearly define the service obstacle and its impact on service.
- Assign the service obstacle to the appropriate area for solution.
- Track and communicate the status of the service obstacle and solution.
- Communicate the solution to all appropriate parties.
- Ensure implementation of the solution.

Figure 10.2 shows the obstacle input screen from the online Service Obstacle System used by Cummins. Because they have operations located around the world, they wanted a system in which any of their business units could not only submit service obstacles, but could also research solutions that may have been developed by other business units. While each division has its own nuances in using the system, the central intranet tracking tool is the system's hub.

Jim January, the Service Obstacle System Champion for the Cummins Power Generation business unit, says the system works because they took the time to carefully educate the entire division on its use and also because the division's senior executive is actively involved in the process. After an obstacle is submitted, Jim and his team determine the appropriate department for creating a solution and meet with the leader of that department to discuss the obstacle. A solution team is created (including the submitter of the obstacle) and the obstacle is carefully tracked and reported through solution. Active obstacles are reviewed monthly during the Cummins Power Generation senior staff meeting. Challenges

	Service Obstacle Form
	Created On:
	Created By:
	Log #:
	Current Owner:

*Indicates Mandatory Fields

Service Obstacle Details by Initiator

Obstacle Data	Information Entry Field
Entry Date:	
Obstacle Initiator:	
Obstacle Initiator Phone Number:*	
Department:*	
Location:*	
Obstacle Initiator Business Unit:*	
SOS Leaders:	
Region:	
Obstacle Category:*	
What is the obstacle that is preventing excellent service delivery?* (Please include at least one example and be as specific as possible)	
Please describe the impact of this obstacle on the customer experience/customer business, and/or your ability to service the customer.*	

Figure 10.2 Service Obstacle Form
Reprinted with permission from Cummins.

(Please include at least one example and be as specific as possible)	
Who is the process owner?* (Please be as specific as possible)	
How often does the obstacle occur?*	
Do you have a recommendation to solve the issue?*	O Yes O No
Has any action been taken to mitigate this obstacle?*	O Yes O No

Provide Attachments

Document/Edit History

Figure 10.2 (*Continued*)

are addressed and additional resources provided as needed. Their online obstacle tracking form is shown in Figure 10.3. Through their system, anyone can see what obstacles have been submitted, who's responsible for the solution, and what progress has been made.

Keep in mind that you may have similar systems in place that can be adapted to include customer service issues. Such was the case with LYNX. They had a very successful process in place for their operations employees to report obstacles and it was fondly known as "Nip It In the Bud." The Service Obstacle System subteam saw it as an opportunity to build upon the success of the current system and widen its scope to include all areas of the organization. The software had to be put in place for its expanded use, but it was felt by the subteam that keeping the name "Nip It

Tracking #	Obstacle	Cross BU or Local Power Gen	Originator's Organization	Date of Origin	Date of Reporting	Days Open

Project Status (Per Project Plan)	Owner's Organization	Process Owner	Closure Date	Notes

Figure 10.3 Service Obstacle Tracking
Reprinted with permission from Cummins.

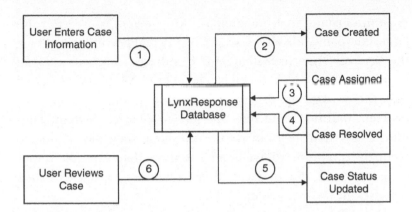

1) User enters concern information from a workstation using the LynxResponse Web interface.
2) Application generates a new case I.D. in the LynxResponse database.
3) Customer Service Counselor assigns the case I.D. to a resource within the LynxResponse database.
4) Assigned resource contacts appropriate entities to resolve the case and enters details in the LynxResponse database.
5) The case status is updated in the LynxResponse database.
6) The user can track the case from a workstation using the LynxResponse Web interface.

Figure 10.4   LYNX "Nip It In the Bud" Process Flow Diagram
Reprinted with permission of Lynx.

In the Bud" and allowing all employees to access the system would be a better approach than totally redesigning a new system for all. Figure 10.4 shows the template and flow of their system.

The Service Obstacle System team will need to work closely with all functions of the organization to test the system and make needed adjustments. They will need to collaborate with those responsible for the Training and Awareness Leadership Actions to ensure that everyone in the organization understands how and when to use the system.

Use of the Formal Service Obstacle System

The formal Service Obstacle System is *not* designed to take the place of local problem solving. Leaders and frontline employees must understand that the company-wide system is used to solve large, company-wide service issues. A very real possibility is to clog the Service Obstacle System with hundreds (or thousands) of issues that should be handled at a local level. We strongly suggest that the workgroup discuss and decide whether or not the problem warrants input into the Service Obstacle System. They may decide that they can resolve the issue themselves and use company communication channels to share their solution. If they cannot resolve the obstacle, then a Service Obstacle System request can be completed.

The obstacle should be submitted in paper or electronic form (such as the one shown in Figure 10.2). The Service Obstacle System subteam determines the appropriate person, department, or team that should be called upon to resolve the obstacle. This is why it is so important for the members of the committee to be well connected and extremely knowledgeable of the inner workings of the organization.

Assigning the obstacles for solution, of course, takes a certain amount of political savvy. Simply turning a problem over to an area for resolution will probably not be very well received. It must be clear that problem resolution is a *collaborative* effort. Experts from appropriate areas of the company must be brought in to help solve such company-wide service issues. While a particular area may need to be at the forefront of a resolution effort, they must understand that the Service Improvement Team, the Service Obstacle System subteam, and the rest of the organization are there to assist.

Tracking the Status of the Service Obstacle

If managed effectively, the Service Obstacle System shouldn't be overwhelmed with issues. In large organizations, however, tracking and reporting progress could be a big job. A tracking mechanism such as the one shown in Figure 10.3 is important to ensure that issues don't drop through the cracks.

Typically, one of the Service Obstacle System subteam members is assigned as the administrator of the tracking mechanism.

Having a single administrator ensures continuity of information. The tracking record provides a common point of reference for use in Service Obstacle System subteam meetings and Service Improvement Team meetings. It is important to also keep the requestor informed of the status regarding the obstacle. People need to know that their input is taken seriously, even though solutions may not be immediate.

Communicate the Solution

We are often surprised to find out that organizations and their customers have endured long-term service problems, only to find out that solutions to the problems had already been determined ages ago. Unfortunately, few people in the organizations knew about the solutions and continued along the path of poor service.

Once a service obstacle has been resolved, the system must "close the loop." We've found that one of the most effective ways to close the loop is to work with the Service Improvement Team member responsible for the Communication Leadership Action. Creating a communication strategy regarding a company-wide service problem/solution should be a collaborative effort between the Service Obstacle System subteam and Service Improvement Team.

Another important point regarding communication: Not all problems will be solved. This is just a fact of organizational life. Part of the success of the Service Obstacle System will rely on not over-promising what it can do. Successes should be communicated throughout the organization, but honest information regarding what may *not* happen is also important to the credibility of the process.

Ensure Implementation of the Solution

Solutions to long-term, company-wide service problems usually take some time to implement. The previous section noted the importance of communicating the solution to the organization. It is just as important to ensure that the solution is indeed implemented and really works! Using their obstacle tracking mechanism, the Service Obstacle System subteam should schedule follow-ups with the requestor and other members of the organization to verify that the solution meets the need. During the implementation process, the Service Obstacle System subteam should maintain a feedback loop with those who developed the solution to the service problem. It's important that, once a problem is solved, it stays solved.

Concluding Thoughts

The purpose of this chapter is to provide a straightforward approach to solving service issues. Don't overcomplicate the process. If you don't *need* an automated tracking system, don't create one. Keep it simple and employees are more likely to use it.

Also, be sure to look outside your own industry for service solutions. Lots of service problems already have some innovative solutions. For example, we've all benefited from the pager system that many restaurants are now using. Instead of having to sit in the restaurant lobby as you wait for a table, the host or hostess gives you a pager so you can wait outside, walk around, or whatever. The pager system has taken away some of the waiting hassle. Many hospitals have also adapted that system for their waiting hassles. While a customer is waiting for a patient that might be having surgery or some other procedure, he or she can now walk outside, go to the hospital chapel, visit the gift shop, and so on. Admissions then pages the customer when any new information comes in. What a great adaptation of a simple idea!

The result of continuous service improvement is happy customers. Employees feel supported and have the opportunity to be service heroes, but the real winner is the customer. If you can solve customer hassles, they will beat a pathway to your door. It takes thought and effort, but it pays off in customer loyalty.

Service Improvement Team Action Steps

- In designing the Service Obstacle System, keep it simple and easy to use.
- Select members for the Service Obstacle System subteam who are well connected and knowledgeable about the inner workings of the organization.
- Create simple, easy-to-use electronic or paper-based input forms for the system.
- Choose an individual or committee who has overall knowledge and authority to become the reviewer of Service Obstacle System requests and assignor of the requests to Service Obstacle System teams.
- Train all employees on the use of the Service Obstacle System.
- Monitor the use of the system to ensure its use.
- Communicate Service Obstacle System successes.
- Be upfront in communicating issues that may not have near-term solutions.

Pitfalls to Avoid

- Don't allow the Service Obstacle System to become the central authority for solving all service issues!
- Don't let the Service Improvement Team start trying to resolve the obstacles. Their role is to develop the system, educate employees on its use, and monitor the process.
- Don't forget to train new employees on the system.
- Don't allow employees to use the system for finger-pointing.
- Don't let Service Obstacle System requests go without response back to the originator.

Chapter Eleven

ACCOUNTABILITY

"I was doing some customer service consulting work with an organization and everything seemed to be going well. Feedback from the field was positive and customers were positively commenting on the overall service attitude. Employees even commented on how much better everyone within the organization treated each other. I really think one of the keys to the success of the initiative was how much the leadership team embraced the importance of holding everyone accountable for delivering great service. Every leader went through a training class that focused on the subject of accountability.

"I did receive a call from one manager who said that this 'customer service thing' wasn't working with his team and that he was disappointed in the initiative. 'Just this morning,' he told me, 'I saw that our receptionist wasn't smiling or greeting customers. Nothing is different than it was before this service initiative.' 'Regarding the receptionist this morning,' I asked, 'what did you do about it?' There was a long pause on the other end of the phone line before his reply, 'I called you.'"

A ccountability is critical to the success of any service improvement initiative. Clearly, the manager in the previous story thought that all he needed to do was send his employees to training and their service performance would magically improve. But, without accountability, service excellence remains a good idea, not a reality. As you can interpret from the content of this book, we advocate building a culture in which people want to provide excellent service. Make no mistake about it, however, there must be mechanisms in place that hold people accountable for their service performance. Without accountability it's easier for employees to just keeping doing things the way they've always done them. In fact, we can confidently state that the number one reason we've seen service initiatives fail to achieve desired objectives is a lack of accountability. Service excellence behaviors must become nonnegotiable.

Keep in mind that the idea of accountability doesn't only apply to leaders holding frontline employees accountable for their performance. It applies to everyone, including the leadership team. As leaders it seems that there are a million things competing for our attention. Which items do we focus on? We focus on those items for which we are held seriously accountable. Many organizations tell employees to do one thing, while management focuses on something completely different. As leaders, we then wonder why our people are so skeptical of new initiatives. Employees are carefully watching their leaders to see if leadership behaviors truly align with stated values.

Accountability is about aligning behaviors with what the organization says it values, pure and simple. Without such alignment of behaviors, values are simply words on a piece of paper. Sometimes accountability comes in the form of penalties for noncompliance (which isn't a bad thing, by the way, as you'll see later). Ideally, however, accountability is about information regarding progress toward fulfilling the company's values. Anything that provides a member of the team with accurate, objective information about performance in relation to company values is valuable.

This chapter will focus on five areas of accountability:

- job descriptions
- attention and focus

- coaching
- promotions
- performance appraisals

Job Descriptions

Every position in the organization should have a job description that outlines key responsibilities, essential job duties, and success measurements. Some job descriptions go into greater detail and include items such as educational requirements, compensation, and growth opportunities. While there are lots of different and effective ways to write job descriptions, our purpose here is to ensure that all job descriptions include customer service criteria.

Job Descriptions for Frontline Positions

Most job descriptions for frontline positions include things like the ability to lift 40 pounds, type 50 words per minute, operate a cash register, fill out order forms, and so on, and they never mention *anything* about customer service. Is it any wonder that employees say, "It's not my job"? Technically they're right if service excellence doesn't appear in the job description!

An ideal approach for developing job descriptions is to use your Service Standards as a framework for describing the majority of employee responsibilities. Some criteria may not fall neatly into the Service Standards and will need to be described under other headings, but the more responsibilities that can be connected to your Service Standards, the better.

Figure 11.1 provides an example of a job description for a full-service gas station attendant (yes, they still exist) based on the Service Standards they had developed. Using their old job description as a starting point, they reformatted it using the Service Standards. During the reformatting process they noticed several customer service gaps in what was expected of employees and added in the behaviors needed to fill those gaps.

Position: Full Serve Attendant
Responsibilities to Serve the Customers:

CORRECT—Ensure that all aspects of the customer interaction are handled and executed correctly.

1. **Adhere to safety regulations.**
   - Adhere to emergency response plan.
   - Adhere to all safety regulations when pumping gasoline.
   - Maintain a safe environment and handle emergencies.
   - Complete a visual check of grounds for snow and ice.
   - Keep driveways, walkways, and pump islands clear of snow and ice.
   - Clean up all spills.
   - Keep lights in good operating condition.
   - Inform manager of any lights not in good working condition or if supply of bulbs is low.

2. **Ensure that all exchanges of products, services, and compensation are fair and accurate.**
   - Pump the amount of gasoline requested by the customer at the full-service island.
   - Accept payment in the form of cash, credit card, debit card, and loyalty card.
   - Provide correct change, receipts, and all appropriate documents that are due to the customer.
   - Answer customer questions with correct information.
   - Provide accurate directions.
   - Recommend car care products (oil, windshield fluid) only when levels are low and in need of replenishment.
   - Complete shift end and balance cash/tender.

3. **Create and present an appropriate image to customers.**
   - Dress in an approved uniform, and present a well-groomed, clean, and fresh appearance at all times.

Figure 11.1   Sample Job Description

- Maintain site exterior cleanliness and orderliness.

- Keep the lot, yard, and pump islands clean and free of debris.

AVAILABLE—Ensure that products, services, and attendant assistance are available to customers when they want and need them.

1. **Ensure that materials and supplies associated with all offerings are stocked and available to customers at all times.**
   - Keep windshield service units stocked and well maintained.
   - Keep washrooms stocked and clean as per site housekeeping schedule.
   - Maintain displays.
   - Keep merchandise clean and stacked neatly in displays.
   - Keep pumps, signs, and glass clean.

2. **Assist customers in obtaining the products and services they want and need.**
   - Acknowledge each driver as they pull into the full-service island with a verbal greeting or a wave.
   - Demonstrate appropriate "hustle," and approach each driver as quickly as possible.
   - Offer to check oil, fluid levels, and to clean windshields.

ATTENTIVE—Look for opportunities to proactively make the customers' experience at the site smooth and hassle-free.

1. **Build relationships with customers by being proactively friendly and helpful.**
   - Proactively engage customer in friendly conversation.
   - Learn regular customers' names, and address them by name when they visit.
   - Sell products that will be of benefit to the customer.
   - Advise customers of any specials or promotions that are being offered inside the store.
   - Thank every customer and invite them back.

Figure 11.1 (*Continued*)

2. Engage customers in participating in loyalty programs and offers.
- Ask customers if they have a loyalty card. If not, explain the benefits of the card and assist them with registration.
- Inform customers of the number of loyalty points they have accumulated, and how their points could be redeemed immediately.
- Advise customers on the best use of loyalty points.

WOW—Exceed customer expectations by providing assistance and service that is "above and beyond" what they expect.

1. Provide special assistance to customers with special needs.
- Offer to obtain products from inside the store for mobility-impaired customers or adults with small children.
- Offer to obtain products from inside the store on rainy days.
- Ask customer if they need any directions before they leave. Provide directions and map when necessary, and obtain directions that you are unsure about.
- Advise customers if tire air pressure seems to need attention and offer assistance in filling tires.
- Be aware of the nearest car repair facilities.

2. Interact with self-serve customers and offer assistance.
- Greet customers at the self-serve pumps.
- Offer "full-serve attention" to self-serve customers whenever the full-service pumps aren't busy.

Creatively solve customer problems, whether site-related or not.

Figure 11.1 (*Continued*)

The descriptors developed for your Service Standards, as described in Chapter 4, can provide a starting point for job description content.

Job Descriptions for Management Positions

The best approach that we've seen for crafting job descriptions for leadership positions is using the popular "three-legged stool" as a guideline. The three-legged stool suggests that leaders should be accountable for three broad areas:

- the customer experience
- the employee experience
- business results

The customer experience section may include such expectations as satisfaction results, retention results, or new products/services introduced. The employee experience section may include items such as turnover rate, training expectations, and employee satisfaction scores. The business results section may include such things as sales goals and cost management. These points, of course, are just examples. The specifics of the job description must depend on the specifics of the job.

Using the three-legged stool approach helps to ensure that balanced expectations are built into a manager's job description. You want managers to create an excellent customer experience, right? You also want managers to select, train, and retain excellent employees. Finally, you want managers to achieve specific business objectives. Spelling out these three areas in job descriptions ensures you don't leave to chance that managers know what's expected of them. This assumes, of course, that managers have seen their job descriptions and that the descriptions are used in the interview, appraisal, promotion, and other accountability processes.

If you find that job descriptions are lacking in customer service elements, you are missing the foundation of the accountability process. Every member of the team, at every level, must know what is expected of them if they are to perform effectively!

Attention and Focus

In most cases, leaders have more control over how they spend their time than frontline employees do. Frontline employees are told specifics like when to work the register, bus the tables, or drive the truck. While leaders *are* pulled in many directions, they can control what they focus on while being pulled. Is it bottom line profitability? Customer service? Employee retention? Granted, no leader's job is easy, but what's paid attention to and focused on in any circumstance is up to the leader.

Your focus and attention regarding the service improvement initiative is critical if the initiative is to work. You can't delegate this focus.

"Our company started using a scorecard for holding managers accountable for balanced performance. We all attended what seemed like a gazillion meetings to hammer out the components of the scorecard. A lot of hours went into creating these things. What a joke. The only thing our VP cared about was the financials. He never even asked about any of the other stuff. If you hit your financial numbers you were golden. If you missed your financial numbers it didn't matter what other factors were strong; you were toast. And everyone knew it."

All levels of leadership must make customer service a priority and demonstrate that priority through behaviors. When you meet with employees, what do you talk about? As you walk the shop floor, what do you comment on? As you interact with customers, what do you ask them?

A manager at a financial institution became an "early adopter" of the company's service improvement initiative. He went through the initial training and enthusiastically brought the information back to his department. One evening he and his fellow managers decorated the entire department to communicate the focus on service. When employees arrived the next day they were blown away by the efforts of their management. They were very proud of being on the leading edge of the initiative. This manager's behaviors demonstrated attention and focus. However, what happened next was *really* interesting. The president of the company heard what this manager had done and made a special trip to the department to see the result and congratulate the team for their efforts. You better believe that word spread quickly throughout the organization that the president paid attention to what this department was doing in regard to service improvement. Other departments started visiting the location and instituting their own support mechanisms. Focus and attention make a real difference.

You need to go beyond individual initiative, however, and implement accountability structures to ensure focus and attention. One such mechanism is management meetings. We've all been in countless meetings secretly planning our retirement to Tahiti or choosing just the right words we'd use to tell the boss what we really think of the meeting. The only time we really pay attention is when someone is talking about our department or when we have to contribute content to the meeting. So make contribution regarding the service initiative a mandatory part of your management meetings. Put service issues first on the agenda. Word will get around about what's important to you.

As a leader, do your direct reports know that you hold them accountable for service excellence? Do you ask your direct reports about satisfaction ratings, customer defection statistics, and employee performance? A hospital CEO we know schedules a hospital walk-through every month with his senior management team. The group is looking for *anything* that detracts from the image of the hospital. The engineering manager has work orders *in hand* as they walk the hospital. You can be sure that attention is focused on getting the noted work done before the next month's walk-through because the CEO will have the previous month's work orders in hand. Some work, of course, requires longer than 1 month to complete, but everyone knows they're held accountable for making sure progress is made. The CEO is also accountable for making on-the-spot decisions regarding resources necessary for the fixes. His credibility is on the line if he's not willing to put forth the resources to create an excellent environment. Everyone's accountable. What do people see you paying attention to?

Coaching

Whenever you see opportunities for improvement for any employee, take the time to coach. Coaching is real-time training and can have a greater impact on actual performance than any seminar or training class.

If, for example, you notice an employee displaying negative physical posture or using a bored tone of voice on the telephone, taking a moment to correct the behavior and stressing *why* it is important to present a welcoming image is more effective in changing behavior than any training program. The *immediacy* of the coaching is the key. Waiting until performance appraisal time to give feedback is not only ineffective in changing behavior, it's unfair to the employee. The question uppermost in an employee's mind when finding out about an ongoing performance problem during an annual appraisal is, "Why didn't you tell me any of this before?"

Oftentimes leaders don't address an employee problem because they're concerned about offending the employee, or the leader is simply uncomfortable with confrontation. But holding employees (at all levels) accountable for service excellence is vital if you are serious about service improvement. Avoiding the situation undermines a leader's credibility and potentially the credibility of the entire service initiative.

"During a hotel stay, I found the service of the staff to be mediocre at best, but nothing to complain about. Except for one employee. She was beyond rude and I found her attitude completely out of line. And it wasn't just me; I saw how poorly she treated everyone she came in contact with. I got her name from her nametag, 'Sarah,' and did something I rarely do—I called the manager to complain. He invited me to have coffee with him in the hotel coffee shop to discuss the problem. He was dismayed by my experience and asked me the employee's name. 'Her name is Sarah,' I replied, 'she works in the gift shop.' 'Oh yeah, Sarah,' he said, 'she's kind of that way.' I couldn't believe it! They *knew* how bad she was and allowed her to keep ticking off the guests!"

Intolerable service exists when intolerable service is tolerated. It's worth reading that line again. When we turn our heads from problem performance, we're actually condoning that performance. We're telling our employees that, while we wish they would treat customers well, it's okay if they don't because there won't be a consequence. "That's just the way she is" really means, "I'm not going to do anything about the problem."

Figure 11.2 provides a process that works extremely well when coaching an employee about a customer service issue. The process sets the tone for the discussion, clearly outlines the problem along with the performance changes expected, outlines the consequences if improvement doesn't occur, and communicates that there *will* be a follow-up discussion. Figure 11.3 is a template that can be used for planning a coaching session so that leaders can go into the discussion fully prepared with what they want to communicate and what outcomes they expect.

Promotions

Countless books and articles make the important point that just because someone is a great salesperson or great technician doesn't mean that person will make a great leader. Effective leadership requires a unique set of skills and talents. We agree completely with this point and won't belabor it here. We will ask, however, who is being promoted in your company? Are they the people who get good business results but leave the bodies of their employees littering the hallways or seeking stress therapy? Are promotions going to the people who don't have the respect of their peers and subordinates? Or are promotions going to those who truly model the values of the organization, while achieving stellar business results? There is probably no single decision that more clearly communicates what an organization values than deciding who gets promoted up the corporate ladder.

A colleague worked for a large organization for many successful years. She led a department that showed stellar customer

1. **Position the discussion**—This step lets the employee know *why* the coaching is occurring. Too often leaders will begin discussing the performance situation (Step 2) without providing context. The best way to position the discussion is to refer to the organization's objectives, values, or standards that connect to the performance issue you are addressing.

2. **Discuss the performance situation**—Based on the perspective of Step 1, what is the current performance? What is happening (or not happening) that is causing a problem? It's important at this step to discuss observable performance and not pass subjective judgments such as, "You have a poor attitude." The best approach is to discuss outcomes that have been agreed upon, but not satisfactorily accomplished or an organizational performance standard that has not been met.

3. **Set a plan of action**—At this step, the employee and the coach agree on what behavior(s) must change. A rule of thumb is that the employee should do the majority of the talking, with the manager guiding the discussion. The employee must own the solution. Keep in mind that the employee will not always agree that there is a performance problem. While it is most helpful that they *do* agree there is a problem, it is more important that they understand you expect a change in performance and that they are clear on what that change is.

4. **Communicate the consequences of non-performance**—This step is often left out because discussing consequences can be uncomfortable for the employee and the manager. Without consequences, however, there is little incentive for the employee to change his behavior. The consequences aren't always extreme, like termination of employment—not every situation is that bad. But consequences must be discussed. The consequence may be to the organization or to the customer experience, but there is always a consequence. The employee should clearly understand the consequences of his or her actions.

5. **Set a follow-up plan**—Pull out the calendar and schedule a follow-up discussion. This step communicates to the employee that the coaching was not just a chat—changes are expected and he will be held accountable for those changes.

Figure 11.2 5-Step Coaching Process for Customer Service Issues (Go to www.UnleashingExcellence.com to download a customizable copy of this form.)

Employee Name:
Step 1: Position the discussion
Step 2: Discuss the performance situation
Step 3: Set a plan of action
Step 4: Communicate the consequences of non-performance
Step 5: Set a follow-up plan

Figure 11.3 Coaching Planning (Go to www.UnleashingExcellence .com to download a customizable copy of this form.)

satisfaction scores, employee satisfaction scores, and had the best financial results in the division (remember the three-legged stool?). The division went through a massive restructure. Our colleague fully anticipated being promoted into a new and expanded key leadership spot. She was not. The person that received the promotion was nowhere near as qualified to lead the new department. The division leader said he was doing "what was right for the business." Our colleague wanted to know how such a decision was right for the business but received no satisfactory answer. Three weeks later she turned in her resignation.

Sounds like sour grapes, right? Our colleague did her research, however. The previous department of the promoted manager had dismal customer satisfaction results that were going nowhere fast. He was not respected by his subordinates or peers and his employee satisfaction scores showed it. Finally, the financial performance of his department was poor at best. Our colleague pointed out these discrepancies to her boss and was told, "You can't really go by those measures." What other measures are there? As we mentioned, our colleague left. The promoted manager lasted another 9 months and was let go during a subsequent restructure. Morale was left in the dust during this time. Think about it: How many times have you seen an undeserving person promoted and then proceed to wreck the morale of a workgroup?

In determining individuals for promotion, be sure to evaluate them on their overall performance in relation to the three-legged stool:

- the customer experience
- the employee experience
- business results

Subordinates and peers will almost certainly respect those who score highly in all three categories. Promoting these high-performing individuals will communicate an important message: "We value each of these factors in this organization." Promoting someone who is weak in one or more of these areas communicates a very different message.

Performance Appraisals

Performance appraisals—how we all hate them. They are the big necessary evil in the accountability process. Any manager who says he loves conducting performance appraisals is either lying or is a masochist. Appraisals take a lot of time and are almost always uncomfortable to give. We will make no promises here that our suggestions will change your opinion or feelings about appraisals. You may still hate them. But if something is going to be painful, it may as well be effective.

Performance Appraisals for Frontline Positions

Because of the typical company structure, many managers conduct *a lot* of frontline performance appraisals. Just for one manager, 20 to 30 appraisals or more on an annual basis isn't unusual, and the situation becomes even more challenging in organizations in which appraisals are conducted every 6 months. We've seen instances in which managers, because of the volume of appraisals they were responsible for, developed a handful of favorite phrases to use in the written section of the appraisal form, trotting out these predeveloped, standard phrases to fit standard situations. One manager we know of even numbered his predeveloped phrases, gave a copy to his administrative assistant, and would simply hand her a page with the appropriate numbers for creating an employee's appraisal. While this manager might get credit for his efficiency, we can't give him any credit for effectiveness.

Performance appraisals are important to employees. In many cases, it's the only opportunity they get to sit down with their leader one on one for any length of time. They also know that the appraisal can impact their pay as well as their chances for advancement. Leaders owe it to their employees to invest time in putting together a thoughtful, complete appraisal.

As in creating job descriptions, using your service standards as a framework for creating a frontline appraisal form is an excellent strategy for hardwiring your service standards into the organizational culture. Figure 11.4 is a section from the Naugatuck Savings Bank performance appraisal. Notice how the majority of the appraisal is structured around their Service Standards of: Safety

Safety and Security		20%
	SCORE	COMMENTS
• Adheres to established procedures as it pertains to locked workstations and logging off the network.		
• Protects privacy of customer information by always locking/securing confidential information.		
• Protects and maintains bank and customer confidentiality.		
• Stays current on policies and procedures.		
• Complies with information tech security policy guidelines and procedures to reduce risks.		
• Completes required annual BVS compliance training.		

Accuracy		20%
	SCORE	COMMENTS
• Accurate balancing and/or processing of work.		

Figure 11.4 Naugatuck Savings Bank Performance Appraisal Service Standards Section

Note: Percentages don't add to 100 percent; other components of the appraisal make up the difference.
Reprinted with permission from Naugatuck Savings Bank.

	SCORE	COMMENTS
• Is able to effectively perform assigned work in the allotted time frames and understands work procedures.		
• Reviews work for completion and accuracy prior to submission.		
• Listens, asks clarifying questions, and provides feedback to ensure accurate understanding of needs.		
• Complies with federal and state regulations and completes forms accurately and on time.		
• Works effectively with minimum supervision.		
• Uses good judgement in absence of detailed instruction, appropriately obtains supervisor's help.		
Responsiveness 20%		
• Answers phone promptly and pleasantly.		
• Assumes responsibility for all work undertaken, follows up on assigned tasks.		

Figure 11.4 (*Continued*)

	SCORE	COMMENTS
• Outputs work in quantities necessary to meet department needs.		
• Offers prompt and accurate responses to requests, inquiries, questions and concerns.		
• Completes work in allotted time, meets deadlines.		
• Has learned the appropriate level of knowledge for time in this position to effectively perform job.		
• Helps other team members when assistance is needed.		
• Uses ingenuity in creating solutions for problems.		

Friendly, Personalized Service 20%

	SCORE	COMMENTS
• Smiles and greets internal/external customers.		
• Understands and responds to the needs of the customer. Strives for "WOW" level of service.		
• Recognizes and routinely demonstrates the importance of looking through the "lens of the customer."		

Figure 11.4 (*Continued*)

• Maintains a pleasant, helpful attitude in overcoming difficulties and obstacles.			
• Routinely performs the Everything Speaks Checklist.			
• Modifies behavior and approach in dealing with different situations.			
• Participates with staff to determine ways to continuously improve customer satisfaction and ensure department goals are met.			

Figure 11-4 (*Continued*)

and Security, Accuracy, Responsiveness, and Friendly, Personalized Service.

Other areas of performance will likely be included in your appraisal form, but be sure that the elements of your service initiative are significantly represented.

Performance Appraisals for Management Positions

While the term "management by objectives" has gone out of vogue, the MBO approach to performance appraisals still yields the greatest results. If appraisals are a look in the rear view mirror only, with no guidance regarding what to look for, it's no wonder that many appraisals are close to useless. On the other hand, if the appraisal system is used to assist managers in setting specific, measurable, and *relevant* goals and help track progress toward those goals, then the system becomes a useful tool for all involved.

The three-legged stool approach to management performance appraisals is effective. At the beginning of the year the manager and his or her leader agree on three to four specific, measurable goals under each of the three categories of the customer experience, employee experience, and business results. This provides a total of 9 to 12 goals that the manager is held accountable for. Please make sure that *customer service* goals are strongly reflected. The rest of the appraisal depends upon your organization's preferred system and may include ratings on specific leadership competencies, developmental goals, and so on.

One company we know of migrated to such an approach a few years ago and it was amazing how things started getting done because "it's on my performance appraisal." Leaders knew that they would be accountable for delivering on objectives under each category and that bonuses and promotions would be based on performance around these agreed upon goals. Not that everyone loved the system. Sometimes, as the end of the year approached, many would bemoan why they set a certain objective on their plan. But they would do everything in their power to achieve the objective!

Performance Objectives		
Develop a minimum of 3 personal objectives for each category. Personal objectives should be linked to corporate and business unit objectives.		
Objectives	Accomplishments/ Feedback	Rating
Customer Experience Corporate Objectives: Business Unit Objectives: Personal Objectives:		
Employee Experience Corporate Objectives: Business Unit Objectives: Personal Objectives:		
Operational/Financial Results Corporate Objectives: Business Unit Objectives: Personal Objectives:		

Rating Scale: E=Exceeds Expectations; M=Meets Expectations; B= Below Expectations

Figure 11.5   Sample Performance Objectives Section of Management Performance Appraisal (Go to www.UnleashingExcellence.com to download a customizable copy of this form.)

Figure 11.5 is an example for structuring the goals section of a management performance appraisal. As with the frontline appraisal, you'll have other performance elements on the form, such as leadership competencies, but structuring the appraisal around the three-legged stool is an excellent way to hold leaders accountable for balanced leadership performance.

When All Else Fails

Some people don't get the hint. You do all that you can to create a culture in which everyone is energized about excellent service. There will always be those, however, who refuse to get on the bus. Those individuals can make everyone's lives miserable, especially if the "non-rider" is in a leadership position. What do you do?

As children, we all promised ourselves that we would never say certain things that our parents said to us, such as, "Because I said so!" or "because I'm the parent and you'll just have to do it as long as you live under my roof!" Later in life, when we have our own children, we all find ourselves saying some of these same things (and it secretly feels good). Why do we sometimes end up saying "Because I said so"? Sometimes it's the only way to get the necessary behavior from our sons or daughters. And so it is in business. Management theorists (like child psychologists) have made us all afraid of offending someone by saying, "Because I said so." And we end up with a nonperforming employee, disillusioned fellow employees, and our own ulcers. There are those employees, frontline and management, who need an ultimatum. Either get on the bus or it's time to move on. And if these individuals don't get on the bus and have no intention of ever getting on the bus, show them to the door.

A CEO of a mid-sized organization we are acquainted with agonized over what to do about one of his top executives. This executive had been with the company for 17 years and had become a friend of the CEO. The CEO recognized that, in order for his company to achieve the next level of performance, teamwork and service would have to play a prominent role and would require a change in the behaviors of everyone in the company, especially the executive team. This long-time executive refused to buy in and became quite divisive in the organization. He sometimes played one member of management against another and caused frustration for everyone. After lots of coaching, he still didn't change. The CEO made the agonizing decision to let this formerly effective executive go. He knew that the change effort didn't stand a chance with one of his key lieutenants actively derailing the process.

When all else fails it's okay to say, "As long as you are under my roof . . ."

Concluding Thoughts

Accountability is a critical component of the service improvement process. So many times we've seen organizations hold a customer service initiative kickoff rally, send hundreds or thousands of employees through service training, and then never hold anyone accountable for service-oriented behaviors. Employees and managers who work hard to embrace the change see no consequences for those who do not. Employees hear their leaders talk about how important service is, and then see those same leaders walk right by a customer who clearly needs assistance.

Accountability mechanisms help to ensure that behaviors match stated values. As you review the stated values of your organization, how are people held accountable for demonstrating those values in practice? How are leaders held accountable for leading service excellence?

Service Improvement Team Action Steps

- Review and revise all job descriptions to include the organization's Service Standards.

- Review and revise all management job descriptions to balance responsibilities regarding the customer experience, employee experience, and business results.
- Work with the Training and Education champion to develop leadership training modules focused on coaching skills.
- Ensure that the organization's succession planning process includes customer service criteria.
- Review and revise all performance appraisals to include customer service elements.
- Ensure that all other performance management tools, such as merit pay structure, include customer service criteria.
- Pay attention to and recognize the "early adopters" of the service initiative.
- Use the "three-legged stool" approach to management accountability.

Pitfalls to Avoid

- Don't let naysayers, especially in leadership positions, poison the service initiative.
- Don't promote individuals who do not model the values of your organization.
- Don't ignore substandard service performance—address the issue immediately. Intolerable service exists when intolerable service is tolerated.

Conclusion

While excellent customer service is something we all wish to incorporate within our organizations, implementing a culture that provides this level of service is a challenging task. Our intent in writing *Unleashing Excellence* was to help guide you through the journey, and it is a journey. Creating a sustained culture of customer service excellence has no end. Behaviors, systems, and processes require daily nurturing and care.

Every organization is different, and there is no cookie-cutter service improvement approach that can simply be plugged into an organization. The process needs to be adapted to the corporate culture. The purpose of this second edition was to provide you with additional tools and examples that we have seen clients use over the years as they have implemented the service improvement process from the book's first edition. By showing ways various clients have applied the Leadership Actions, we hope you are inspired to adapt these principles to your own organization.

As you move forward with the service improvement process, be sure to keep things simple. Our experience demonstrates that many organizations are likely to overcomplicate any initiative they tend to take on, including service improvement initiatives. These organizations analyze everything to death and end up paralyzed, too overwhelmed to do anything. The approach recommended within these chapters is designed to be relatively simple and straightforward. Whether you are a small business or large business, the principles are the same; it's only the scope that changes. Whereas a large organization may pull a team together to plan and implement a Leadership Action, a small organization may just assign the task to one person. The key is to keep it simple and remember the intent of each action. In summary, let's briefly review those intents and the call to action that accompanies each.

Leadership Action 1: Create the Service Improvement Team

This action identifies a core group of people who will lead the service improvement initiative efforts. Their commitment and dedication to the process is vital to its success. Make sure you carefully select these team members and continually remind them of the important role they play.

Leadership Action 2: Develop the Organization's Service Improvement Core Tools

The outcome of this action becomes the heart of the entire service process. It identifies the purpose of the organization for all employees and clearly defines the guidelines for their behaviors. The Service Philosophy and Service Standards become the stake in the ground for all future improvement efforts. The Everything Speaks Checklist and Service Mapping tools will provide the mechanisms for quickly raising the bar on your current service levels.

Leadership Action 3: Develop and Execute an Ongoing Service Communication and Awareness Plan

This action recognizes the need to constantly keep the importance of delivering excellent service in the forefront of employees' daily activities. With all the information bombarding people today, it is hard to know what should be paid attention to the most. Keep this Leadership Action fun, interesting, and informative, so everyone in the organization will look forward to seeing and hearing what's new or happening in regards to service improvement.

Leadership Action 4: Create and Execute a Plan for Ongoing Service Training and Education

What sets this training apart from many other initiatives are two things:

All employees at all levels go through training.

The service concepts remain the same, but their application is different depending upon the roles and responsibilities of each level.

Make certain everyone attends their appropriate education session. Design the training sessions to be entertaining enough so that everyone will look forward to their turn to go to the class.

Leadership Action 5: Adapt the Interviewing and Selection Process to Include All Elements of the Service Culture

This Leadership Action ensures your organization will not bypass the most impressionable time in a potential new employee's introduction to your business. This period of time is critical to communicating the service culture desired. It allows both the organization and the potential new hire the opportunity to decide if there is a right fit in not only job tasks, but also in service attitudes.

Leadership Action 6: Create and Implement a Service Measurement Process

When implementing this action, the organization is communicating to everyone how serious management is about improvement. We all know that those things of most importance in business are things that can be measured. Keep the focus on improvement rather than placing blame.

Leadership Action 7: Develop Appropriate Recognition/Celebration Processes that Reinforce the Service Culture

Recognition and appreciation will go a long way in building momentum and enthusiasm for your service improvement initiative. Not only will this Leadership Action institute a process of celebration for achievement and participation, but it will also be a daily reminder of the importance of how to treat people. Keep recognition sincere, simple, and creative.

Leadership Action 8: Implement a Service Obstacle System for Identifying and Addressing Barriers to Service Excellence

The ability to deliver excellent service is not always entirely in the hands of the frontline employees. Sometimes their ability to deliver service excellence is affected by the systems and processes they are given to work with. This Leadership Action provides the opportunity for employees to identify and communicate those obstacles that get in the way. The system is designed to be straightforward, nonthreatening, and easy to use. Be sure you are ready to start taking corrective action when you institute this Leadership Action!

Leadership Action 9: Build a Management Accountability System that Ensures Commitment to Ongoing Service Excellence

The keyword in this action is *ongoing.* Improvement initiatives get started all the time; however, few have the sustainability to become engrained in the culture. In the final analysis, account-ability is the key differentiator between successful initiatives and those that are not so successful. Be steadfast in the development and monitoring of an accountability system, as over time it will ensure the other eight Leadership Actions will become an inte-grated part of your organization.

Final Thoughts

Changing a culture takes time. It requires positive and constructive reinforcement to keep going in the right direction. It's easy to get off track and slip back into the old way of doing things. We live in a society that wants change to happen instantly. We want to see immediate results from our efforts. Lasting change doesn't work that way. Patience is required.

Significant changes will take place and progress will occur, but the icing on the cake manifests itself down the road in 3 to 5 years. This delay is why most organizations begin and abandon one improvement program after another. It is challenging and it takes time. Those organizations that stick with it are the ones that become world-class. The clients mentioned in this book will all tell you that there were times when they too doubted and questioned the time and effort put into the process. However, those who have stayed focused and committed will agree it has made a change in how they do business and their customer satisfaction measurements show the improvement.

Use *Unleashing Excellence* as the "how to" book for getting started. You can literally begin with Leadership Action 1 and start by putting together the Service Improvement Team. The second step will be to develop the Service Improvement Core Tools. From that point, you can then just follow through on the other Leadership Actions as you begin to implement the tools that are described in this book. Most everything you will need to truly implement a culture of service excellence is contained herein. Feel free to use the forms and ideas as benchmark platforms to design what will work best for your organization. Tailor the concepts to fit and enhance what you are already doing to improve your customer service. Hopefully, ideas have been mentioned in the book that have already triggered you to notice things in your organization that you've never noticed before. That's good, because awareness is the first step toward improvement. Recognize that awareness will not occur for everyone at the same time, as demonstrated in the following scenario:

Three employees were once asked by their supervisor to make sure they delivered great service with every transaction. The first employee countered with the question, "So, what do you want me to do, Boss, great service *or* my job?" The second employee, when given the same directive responded, "So, you want me to do great service *and* my job?" The third employee, upon being told the requirement, simply replied, "But great service *is* my job!" How would your employees respond?

We wish you the best of luck in your efforts. Let the journey begin!

Index

Note: page numbers in italics indicate illustrations